History of Wallasey
1800-1939

P. Davies

To my family and friends.

Thank you.

The Mill on the Breck

INDEX

Chapter 1 The Transition Period 1800-1850	6
Wallasey in 1811	7
The Townships of Wallasey	8
Wallasey Village	8
The Township of Poulton-cum-Seacombe	13
Poulton Village	14
Seacombe Village	16
The Township of Liscard	18
Liscard Village	18
The Powder Magazines	20
Mother Redcap's	22
Liscard Moor	23
Chapter 2 The Enclosure Acts	25

The Wallasey Ship Canal	34
Chapter 3 Wallasey From 1831-1851	38
William Rowson	45
Distribution of Land-Holders and Settlements in 1846	48
Chapter 4 Wallasey From 1851-1914	58
Growth of Population 1851-1911	58
The Development of Communications	61
The Four-Fold Character of Wallasey	70
Chapter 5 Progress in Local Government	85
Chapter 6 Wallasey In The Post War Years 1914 - 1939	91
The Population of Wallasey	91
Movements of Workers and Occupations	95
Extension of The Borough and The Problems of Housing	109
Chapter 7 Wallasey in The Post War Years – 1918-1939	118
The Origins and Development of the Moreton 'Caravan Town'	118
The Post-War Development of New Brighton	125
The Provision of Public and Private Services and Amenities	128
Other books by the author	137

Chapter 1

The Transition Period

1800 - 1850

During the nineteenth century Wallasey's growth was principally based upon the growth of Liverpool as the commercial and industrial centre of north of England. The influence of people from Liverpool had yet been unfelt at the beginning of the nineteenth century. The Wirral, generally speaking, was very thinly peopled; few townships having more than 250 people per 1000 acres. This was partly the result of its relative isolation, owing to the marshes of the Growy and Broxton Valleys at the southern end of the peninsula, and partly because of the large proportion of thinly soiled sandstone upland forming mainly heaths. The people were almost wholly agriculturalists and the only township of any importance was that of Neston with Parkgate (105 people per 100 acres) which combined with its local agriculture and coal mining the three-fold character of a market-town, a port with a small trade especially with Ireland, and a sea-side resort.

Early view of Wallasey Pool. St. Luke's Church steeple can be seen on the ridge.

Wallasey in 1811

Situated at the north-east extremity of the Wirral lies Wallasey which was still further isolated by its position and above all, by the presence of Wallasey Pool and the marshes on its southern and westerly borders. There was also a lack of any important roads to and from Wallasey. Consequently, its population had remained very small totaling in 1801 some 663 in all as compared with 355 in 1545, and 345 in 1663. The Township of Liscard contained 23 people per 100 acres and the Township of Poulton-cum-Seacombe and Wallasey 21 and 17 respectively. At the time of the 1811 Census the population of the Parish had increased to 943 made up of 440 in Wallasey. 239 in Liscard, and 214 in Poulton-cum-Seacombe. As in the Wirral, the inhabitants were mainly engaged in agriculture although certain other activities were carried on such as fishing.

An early painting of Seacombe, 1820

The settlements in the Wallasey area at this time consisted of the four villages or hamlets of Wallasey, Liscard, Poulton and Seacombe, the sites of which were partly controlled by relief and partly by their position in relation to the Mersey crossing and that across the Wallasey Pool. These villages had slowly grown up on the elevated eastern part of the Parish where, in general, the low plateau was favoured by :-

1. a relatively dry site, especially when the villages were on the sandstone outcrop uncovered by glacial drift as in the case of Wallasey Village and Poulton;
2. the open heath character favoured building;
3. the relief and the bordering marshlands and Wallasey Pool afforded protection from land invaders;
4. water supply - wells and springs in the sandstone provided clear and pure water in contrast with the polluted, standing water of the "Moss" or marshes;
5. proximity to the clayey lowlands of the "Moss" or Wallasey Pasture that provided land for pasture, whilst the lighter soils at the junction of the clay and the sand gave soil suitable for arable farming.

The Townships of Wallasey

Wallasey Village

In 1811 Wallasey Village consisted of some 94 families totaling 440 people who lived in 68 houses. Most of these house or cottages were situated on either side of a long straggling street which began just below Wallasey Church at the junction with School Lane, and extended northwards to Green Lane; others bordered School Lane. Nearly all these cottages or small farmsteads, nestling at the foot of the Parish Church or the lower slope of St. Hilary's ridge at an average elevation of about 45 feet, were sufficiently high up to avoid the flooding of the "Moss" in heavy rains and high tides. The houses were largely made from the local sandstone, usually of squared blocks of the yellow-grey Keuper Basement Beds obtained nearly in the Brake or Breck or Breck Quarry, laid in courses and with slated roofs. In addition, there were several picturesque snow-white cottages with roofs of straw thatch. These represented an older type of house that was constructed by setting up "crucks", which were roughly hewn tree trunks or large boughs leaning against each other to meet at the top, a cross-piece supporting them half-way up, thus forming something like a capital "A". These crucks, placed about sixteen feet apart, and connected by the ridge pieces, purlins and numerous braces, formed the skeleton of a dwelling, which was completed by filling in the sides with "cob". i.e, clay with straw trodden into it, or else with rough masonry or brick-work, and roofing with thatch. This kind of cottage was generally long and low, often of only one storey, though an upper room under the high-pitched roof was not uncommon. One of these types of old cottages existed in Liscard Village, opposite the Delivery Post Office, known as Egerton Cottages.

Cheshire Cheese, c1880

The Inns of the Village were both of sandstone construction, namely, the Old Cheshire Cheese at the foot of St. Hilary Brow and the Black Horse (1722) which took its name from a certain horse famous in the annals of the Wallasey Races. Both of these Inns, of course, are now reconstructed.

This settlement in Wallasey Village dates back to very early times and reference is made to it in Domesday (1086). Its name is probably derived from "Wealas-ey", the island of the Welshmen or strangers, in that, by its inaccessibility, it formed a refuge for the early inhabitants from the invading Saxons. The village grew up in close proximity to the Parish Church of St. Hilary which stands on the crest of the ridge just to the east.

The earliest church was probably of wood or of wattle and daub and the Scandinavian name of the parish Kirby would imply that it existed at the time of the Norse invasion in the 6th century.

Black Horse, c1880

Remains of a Norman Church of the 11th and 12th centuries have been traced and later, in 1520, the sandstone tower that stands today in the churchyard, was built in very late Perpendicular style, embattled, with gargoyles, and corner buttresses, and coarse three-light belfry windows. With the exception of this tower the Church, was pulled down in 1760 and re-built, remaining with certain additions until destroyed by fire on 1st February, 1857. Close to the Church was the refectory, built of stone in 1672, and the old Wallasey Hall, built by W. Meols in 1602 and demolished about the middle of last century.

Adjoining the houses on either side of Wallasey Village, were the barns and shippons standing usually in a yard, beyond which on the western side, the small crofts or closes were separated by the lower part of School Lane or the "Gutter", from the meadows that sloped down to a small stream draining southwards to Wallasey Pool. Beyond this stream, and extending to the western and northern limits of the Parish were the open, unenclosed lands called the Wallasey Leasowe and Wallasey Pasture lying north and south respectively of an ancient boundary fence, in which most of the land-holders had common rights. Running westwards across the Leasowe and providing the main land outlet was a narrow lane (Green Lane) which led to the extreme westerly part of Wallasey Parish where stood the New Hall or as it was better known, Leasowe Castle. The tower of this Hall or Castle was probably built by the 5th Earl of Derby in 1593, possibly in connection with the horse-racing on the Wallasey shore but more likely as a refuge or protection (the walls are over three feet thick) which the disturbed conditions of his time made desirable. It was also in an excellent position for watching the sport of hawking, standing in the midst of an extensive open plain. Several additions were made during the early part of the 17th Century but following upon the suppression of "wordly sports and pastimes" by the Puritans of the Commonwealth period it probably was deserted and became known as Mockbeggar Hall. At the end of the century it was used as a farm house and during the 18th Century it was occupied by various people including Mr. Egerton (1772-1786) and Robert Harrison who sold it in 1802 to Mrs. Boode when it was first called Leasowe Castle. Its subsequent history can be summarised as follows :-

- 1825 converted into a hotel by Sir Edward Cust, husband of Mrs. Boode's daughter. Unsuccessful.
- 1843-79 Sir Edward Cust lived there at spasmodic intervals. Additions and improvements made including the panelling of the library with bog oak from the submerged forest, the panelling of the dining-room with oak from the Star Chamber at Westminster, and the construction of the so-called Battle staircase.
- 1895 Again converted into a hotel by a private Company.
- 1910 Purchased by the Trustees of the Railwaymen's Convalescent Homes and opened as such in 1911 remaining so until the First World War when it housed German prisoners
- 1970 Opened as a restaurant and hotel

The northern margin of the Leasowe passed into the belt of sand hills which extended eastward into the waste lands in the Township of Liscard, known as Liscard Common.

East of Wallasey Village, extending approximately from Back Lane or Middle Lane (now St. George's Road) to the Liscard Boundary and bounded southwards by the ancient road heading from Wallasey Village to Liscard Common and Village (now Wallasey Road) were the old enclosed lands made up of the arable fields running up the hillside in long, narrow strips to Top Lane (now Claremount Road) and still further eastwards, more narrow and irregularly shaped patches of land in the old Town Fields. In the Tithe Maps of Wallasey in 1841 these are shown practically unchanged.

South of Wallasey Church, and bordering along the crest of the ridge the eastern side of the old road leading to the village of Poulton (now Breck Road) was the narrow strip of open waste land known as Wallasey Brake or Breck which contained the main quarry for the local stone. Between 1752 and 1814 the Wallasey inhabitants had been encroaching upon this open land but it was not until the latter date that the formal enclosure took place. In the Breck stood Wallasey School, the predecessor of the Grammar School in Withens Lane which later moved to Moreton. In some form a grammar school has existed from as early as 1654, if not earlier. After existing for over a century (1856-1799) the original school, probably under the same roof as the Church, was pulled down and the new one on the Breck constructed by public subscription. Close to the school stood Wallasey Mill, high up on the hill and so exposed to the full force of the prevailing westerly winds. This was built of stone in 1765, on or near the site of an earlier mill.

The inhabitants of Wallasey Village and Township, as already mentioned, were mainly engaged in agricultural pursuits. According to the 1811 Census 65 out of the total 94 families were dependent on agriculture, 16 on trade, manufactures and handicrafts, and the remainder on other unspecified occupations. There can, however, be little doubt that these occupations were supplemented on a considerable scale by the villainous practices of wrecking and smuggling which were favoured by the position of

Wallasey in regard to the shipping of the Mersey and the difficulties of navigation owing to the presence of numerous sand-banks at the entrance to the river. James Stonehouse, writing in 1863 states:

> "Wirral at that time and the middle of last century was a desperate region, the inhabitants were nearly all wreckers and smugglers. They ostensibly carried on the trade and celling of fisherman, farm labourers, and small farmers, but they were deeply saturated with the sin of covetousness and many a fierce fire has been lighted on the Wirral shore on stormy nights to lure the good ship on the Burbo or Hoyle Banks, there to beat, strain and throb until her timbers parted and her planks were floating in confusion on the stormy waves".

Smuggling, too, was very rampant especially in brandy, gin, rum, salt and tobacco but this was carried on chiefly in the Township of Liscard where suitable landing and hiding places were to be found at Mother Redcap's, the Magazines, and the Red Noses

The Township of Poulton-cum-Seacombe

This Township, the smallest of the three in the Parish, lay to the south of those of Wallasey and Liscard. Its eastern border was the River Mersey and to the south and south-west was Wallasey Pool. Unlike the other Townships it had two distinct settlements, Poulton Village in the west and Seacombe Village in the south-east. Both were small hamlets with a total number of inhabited houses given as 38 in 1811. The combined population was 214 comprising some 42 families of which 15 were engaged in agricultural, only 4 in trade, manufacturers, and handicrafts, with the remaining 23 devoted to other activities. Here then, in contrast to Wallasey and Liscard, agriculture was not the outstanding occupation although very important. From the position of the two hamlets it is very probable that the greater part of the 23 families engaged in unspecified activities, were concerned with fishing or with the ferries across the Mersey and Wallasey Pool.

Poulton Village

Pool Inn and the pinfold, 1841

Poulton Village, taking its name from the "Ton" or hamlet, on the "Pool", had grown up near the ferry across the Pool. In the Vyner Map of Poulton, circa 1665, this ferry is shown as being situated at the end of Limekiln Lane near the western side of Hooks Common but it is possible that an earlier ferry existed inland nearer the head of the Pool by Poulton Common (close the site of Poulton Bridge). This would probably be a ferry about high water and a ford when the tide was out. Neither of these ferries is shown on the Enclosure Map of 1823 but an embankment is marked running from the Common probably on the site of the earliest ferry. This was erected about 1809 by Robert Vyner, Lord of the Manor of Wallasey, to connect his lands in Bidston with those in Poulton. The Village itself, a little away from the Pool to avoid flooding and standing on the Keuper Sandstone (Basement Beds) outcrop at an elevation of about 40 to 50 feet, was at the junction of

Rake Lane (now Breck Road), Mill Lane, the ancient road leading to Seacombe (now Poulton Road), and Limekiln Lane. In the Village were several stone-built cottages or houses including one that stands today, the oldest, apart from Leasowe Castle.

This is 'Bird's House' and is situated at the junction of Poulton Bridge Road and Limekiln Lane, which has the date and initials as seen in the picture on the left. The initials stood for William Bird (with a difference of opinion that the date is either 1621, 1627 or 1697) and it was carved on the front door lintel. William was a yeoman who lived here, but it is hard to say which member of the family built the house. Richard Bird's son was born on 3rd September 1577 and another William Bird on 8th November 1599. Woods & Brown book, 'The Rise and Progress of Wallasey', believe the date to be 1697. They point out that the accounts of for the Church warden at St. Hilary's Church for the year 1658 are signed by William Bird. Close at hand were the old circular-walled pinfold which housed stray cattle and the old Pool Inn, situated a little south of the rebuilt one which in turn was closed in 2010 and soon after demolished.

The outstanding buildings, however, were Poulton Hall, a large four-square brick-built house that replaced the old Hall about 1790-1800, and Poulton Manor House, another fine brick house built about the same time. No mill is shown on the 1823 map but the Vyner Map (1665) marks one at the bottom of Mill Lane close to the present St. Luke's Church. This unlike the Wallasey Breck Mill (100 feet above sea-level) was at a relatively low level (about 50 feet) but as the low-lying Bidston and Wallasey marshes extended to the west from which direction most of the winds came it would not be a very great handicap.

Just to the west of the Village was the small Common which remained open, like the other commons and waste lands of the Township, until the Commissioner's Awards of 1823. Eastwards stretched the old-enclosed arable and pasture lands across which an old lane (Poulton Road) led to Seacombe Common and Seacombe Village.

Extending southwards from the western part of Seacombe Common, was Seacombe Dale (now marked as Oakdale Road), the combe from which probably Seacombe derived its name. Between the Dale and the ferry end of Lime-Kiln Lane and bordering the strand or shore of Wallasey Pool was The Hooks Common (noted as No 257/258 on a 1841 Tithe Map), a low-lying marsh land with several small creeks and liable to overflowing by Spring tides but no doubt providing excellent pasture.

Seacombe Village

Seacombe Village consisted of a few houses in the neighbourhood of the Seacombe Ferry to Liverpool, which was then situated at the bottom of Church Road. Later all the land south east of a line running approximately from the old Seacombe Ferry Hotel to the bottom of Kelvin Road would be reclaimed and the ferry re-sited There is no concrete evidence available of the original site of Seacombe Village and Ferry but the mention of ferries across the Pool, and the name Seacombe render it quite possible that the settlement and the ferry were situated near the head of the numerous creeks which branched from Wallasey Pool between Poulton and the Mersey, a position more sheltered and therefore more suitable for the small boats which plyed until the nineteenth century. The earliest reference to a ferry is quoted by Stewart Brown from the Chester Plea Rolls :-

> "... they were the lords of the town of Secum and therefore had the right of passage across the Mercee and could load and unload their boats at Waleyespull and between Waleyespull and Ranildespull either in Claughton or in Secum".

Various references to Seacombe Ferry occur from then onwards but no evidence is forthcoming as to when the Ferry was established near the bottom of Church Road. At this time (1811) as throughout the 18th Century, the service was very irregular and primitive. The boats were small, either single or double masted, and landing consisted in wading or being carried ashore. According to William Moss, 'Stranger In Liverpool', in 1797, the charge was "twopence for market people and common passengers ... and sixpence is generally expected from the upper order of passengers".

Close to the Ferry was the hotel or inn which a little later in the century became fashionable. Access to and from the Ferry was by means of a track or road across Seacombe Common to the junction of Liscard Road and Poulton Road which roads or lanes led to Liscard and Poulton respectively.

Seacombe Ferry, c1850. Seacombe Hotel left centre and Marine Hotel extreme left.

Away from the Village, close to the entrance of the Wallasey Pool to the Mersey, was the Smalt Works of Mawdsley and Smith, the only industrial works shown on the Enclosure Map of 1823 and the predecessor of the important and commercial activities of those part of modern Wallasey. It is possible, however, that the Copper Works of John Bibby, Sons and Company, were already in existence. Woods and Brown state that these were founded in 1812 and existed until about 1863. They are not shown on the 1823 Map but appear on the 1841 Map near Creek Side, off Dock Road.

The Township of Liscard

This Township, lying to the north of Poulton-cum-Seacombe Township and west of Wallasey, occupied the eastern and north-eastern part of the Parish. In 1811, the total population was 289 composed of some 54 families who lived in 51 houses. The greater part of these families were dependent upon agriculture, as was the case in Wallasey Township, 40 of the 54 families being engaged in that activity while 7 of the remaining 14 were occupied in trade, manufacturers, and handicrafts. The activities of the final 7 are not given but would include those concerned with the Magazines (as will be discussed in 'The Powder Magazine'), and the supplying of food and liquor to the sailors who frequented the Pilot Boat Hotel, and the Magazine Hotel as well as Mother Red Caps.

Liscard Village

The old and the new. The old Boot Inn is seen in front of the newly built pub, 1925.

Liscard Village consisted mainly of a few cottages or houses with their yards and crofts, situated on the drift-covered, low plateau at an elevation of approximately 100 feet near the junction of the present Wallasey Road, Seaview Road, Rake Lane and Liscard Road. The original site is not definitely known but Henry Robinson in his account of Wallasey written in 1727, says "... there was a great man call'd Lee who had Kirk situated near the westward of the Kirkway, --- and his town stood near the Kirk... Mr G(l)over said that the right name of Liscard was Liskirk, this Lee, whose Mansion House was that of John, Als Long Young ..." If this "Lees Kirk" - which may have been an oratory, served by Birkenhead Priory - ever existed at all, it probably was near the top of Earlston Road, by the present Kirkway, in which case the older house built into the present children's section of Earlston Library is possibly the Mansion House mentioned by Robinson - 'Rose Bank' (later known as Earlston House). At the other end of the present Kirkway, on the edge of Liscard Common, was the windmill standing in an exposed position on the highest portion of the Township. Bearing in mind the statements of Robinson there is little reason to suppose that the original nucleus of Liscard Village was very far from its position in 1811. As in the other Villages, the houses were mainly of sandstone construction obtained from the Keuper Basement Beds quarried on Liscard Common at the junction of the present Rake Lane, Upper Rowson Street, and Magazine Lane (Quarry Recreation Ground). Good examples of this type, now demolished, were Urmson's House (1729-1928) opposite the car park in Liscard Village (where previously there had been a Fire Station), the Blue Bell Inn which once stood next to the Fire Station with the turf roof covered with a luxuriant growth of grass up to about 1899, and Liscard Hall Farm standing on the site of the present Royal Mail Delivery Office. In addition, a little west of the Village and on the edge of Liscard Moor, was the old "Boot" Inn, of Elizabethan times, which is generally supposed to take its name from the old boot preserved traditionally in connection with the following legend :-

> "Our good Queen Bess did rule this realm, when honest Jack was hoaste unto this Inn, well helped by lusty wife and bucksome daughter Joan. One wild dark night when all were snoring snug abed, a fierce wild horseman bedaubed with muck and blood, did gallop to the door, making a thunderous thump thereon, when our hoaste did open untoe him, he rushed intoe the house, a big jack boot in one hand, and a great pistol in t'other, calling wild foul words for instant meat and drink. He had a beastly savage look, and our hoaste did eye him well while meat and drink went down his wolfish maw. Thinks Jack there's booty in that boot, for when he thumped it on the board there was a chink of gold, the pistol too was bye. Our honest Jack was cute and bolde, and when he turned in wrath Jack whipped the pistol to his sconce and called for lusty wife and bucksome Joan, and they did bind the robber

safe and sure, and made the gold lined boot secure. This scarce was done when in bounced three gentlemen, one with bloody sconce and bootless leg, who when he saw the robber bound was glad, but soon began to wail his boot. Now did our hoaste begin to crow and bid his woman bring the gold lined boot. The gentleman was then in hearty mood and gave then guineas to our hoaste, then more to lusty wife and bucksome Joan. He gave the robber to the gibbet, and the boot to be a sign unto this Inn while it doth stand".

There would be also in the Village several brick-built houses, mostly small and unpretending, and at least two examples of the older type already described.

Eastwards from the Village to the Mersey and extending north and south respectively to Liscard Common, and Liscard Moor and the boundary of Poulton-cum-Seacombe Township, were the old enclosed lands of the freeholders and tenants of Liscard, partly arable lands and partly meadow and pasture lands, rather similar to the clay lands bordering the Dee from below Caldy Hill to Parkgate. Across these fields an old road (now Rake Lane) led northwards to Liscard Common, an open windswept waste largely covered with blown sand except where the sandstone cliffs outcropped on the shore in the neighbourhood of the Red Noses. At this time (1811) a Commissioner was already working on an award in connection with the enclosing of this Common in accordance with the Act of 1809. Running eastwards, along the edge of the Common was a path or lane (now Magazine Lane) leading to the Magazines and the few houses bordering the shore.

The Powder Magazines

The Powder Magazines had been established in this open, isolated area by the Corporation of Liverpool sometime between 1751, when they were removed from Clarence Street, on account of the danger of carting gunpowder through the streets of Liverpool, and 1768 when there was evidence of the lease of this land for the Powder Magazines to William Penkett of Bidston, son of the John Penkett who purchased the Manor of

Liscard in February 1801. In the 1812 Map they are shown as three distinct compartments but later they were reconstructed. Close to the Magazines were the brick-built Pilot Boathouse Hotel (1747) and the Magazine Hotel (1759), both popular "rendezvous" of the sailors of the ships anchored in the offing for the unloading of their powder preparatory to going into dock, or for taking in of their powder before going to sea. Most of the ships carried guns at this time as Britain was engaged in the Napoleonic War and there was also some trade in gunpowder with West Indies. Bordering these Inns were a few stone-built cottages together with barns and cow-sheds the products of which, no doubt, supplied the outward bound ships. About three or four hundred yards southwards along the shore once stood two stone-built cottages, Sea Bank Cottages, and the well-known Mother Red Cap's.

Boys using the Fort entrance as a goal whilst a cannon lays against the old wall to the right, c1912

Mother Redcap's

Mother Redcap's, 1888

Mother Red Cap's was a famous haunt of smugglers and was built about 1595 by a member of the Mainwaring family. The original walls were nearly three feet thick and on the outside were covered with thick planks from wrecked ships. The front door of oak, was five inches thick and studded with square-headed nails and on the inside was a trap-door which precipitated unwary intruders into the cellar some eight or nine feet below. It could also be used for lowering contraband goods to this cellar. Another and larger cellar or cavern existed at the back of the house from which a narrow underground passage led to a concealed opening in a ditch that in turn, ran as far as a pit which was about half-way up the present Lincoln Drive. The entrance to this cavern was in the back-yard where stood a large manure heap, and a stock of coal and coal-scales. This coal was supplied by Flats, and was retailed to the people of Liscard and Wallasey as a blind to the smuggling activities.

Outside, facing the Mersey, was a short wooden flagstaff with a dummy weather-vane used by the smugglers for signaling. When it pointed to the house it meant "Come on" and when pointing away, "Keep off". The smuggled goods were temporarily hidden in and about Mother Red Cap's and then at night secretly removed, and taken along foot-paths and lanes past Liscard Village, and down the present Bidston foot-path to "Hannah Mutche's Farm" at the east end of the "Moss", the main haunt of the smugglers. The house became a tavern in the privateering days of 1778-90 and was frequented by the Officers and crews. About this time it probably became known as Mother Red Cap's from the fact of the owner always wearing a red hood or cap. She became a great favourite with the sailor men and frequently hid them from the Pressgang as well as acting as a depositary for their pay and prize-money until they wanted it.

A short distance away once stood a fine brick-built 18th Century house and it's out houses, and appears in the 1841 Map as Liscard Manor House. The old Manor House was on the site of Earlston Library and no direct evidence is available as to the exact date when the title was transferred to this house. It is known, however, that John Penkett, a Liverpool merchant, had the lease of this house in 1794 when it was called "Sea Bank". In 1801, the same John Penkett purchased all the Manor of Liscard so it may reasonably be presumed that the transference of title took place between 1801 and 1841, probably after 1810.

From Sea Bank or Liscard Manor House, a lane led westwards across the enclosed lands to (Withens) Lane and then via another road (now Urmson Road) to Liscard Village. From here a track or road skirted the edge of Liscard Moor and after passing through a gate at the boundary of the Township, continued on (the present Wallasey Road) to Wallasey Village.

Liscard Moor

Liscard Moor, the remaining open waste land in the Township, lay to the south and south-west of the Village as far as the boundary with Poulton-cum-Seacombe, i.e. as far as the site of the vacant St. John's Church. Across it ran a track or Lane (now Liscard Road) leading towards Seacombe Village and Ferry via Seacombe Common. Around the southern margins of the Moor "squatter" settlements existed and a number of houses and cottages sprawled with a marked concentration along the north side of what is now Withens's Lane. The only outstanding building here was that of the Rev. John Tobin, called Liscard House. It was built by Sir John Tobin for the above-named son, probably about 1833, as the eastward end of the present Chatsworth Avenue which was laid-out on the side of the drive. The owners and lease-holders of the lands bordering the Moor had been encroaching upon it, probably by agreement since 1761, and already by 1811, the Act for enclosing both the Moor and the Common had been passed and the Award was in preparation.

Chapter 2

The Enclosure Acts

The Enclosures of 1809 and 1841

Early in the 19th Century the remaining commons and waste lands in the Parish of Wallasey were enclosed following upon the Acts of 1809 and 1814. The 1809 Act, entitled "An Act for enclosing the Waste Lands in the Township of Liscard", in the Parish of Wallasey, resulted in the enclosure of approximately 408 acres, nearly half the entire area of the Township, made up of the open and uncultivated patches of land called Liscard Moor and Liscard Common. The promoters of the Act were the owners or proprietors of lands and tenements in the Township and as such entitled to rights on the commons and waste lands. Prominent among these land-holders were John Penkett, Esq, Rev. Sir Henry Poole Bart, John Deane, Thomas Molyneux, Gerald Stanley, and several others including the Rev. George Briggs (Rector of Wallasey, 1768-1814), and the Corporation of Liverpool in respect to their holdings in the Magazines. It was claimed that "the said commons and waste lands in their present state are of little value; but if the same were divided and allotted into specific shares unto and amongst the proprietors thereof and persons interested therein, and such allotments enclosed, they would be considerably improved". Accordingly, the Act makes provision for the fencing of the allotments, for defraying the expenses incident to the carrying out of the Act, and for the laying out of roads .Section 26 reads as follows :-

> "And whereas the said commons adjoin chiefly on the coast or shore of the River Mersey, and there is not, nor ever can be, much passing over the public roads to be made in, over, upon or across the commons; be it further enacted that the said Commissioner (James Boydell, of Rossett) shall have, and hereby hath, full power given to him to set out all and every or any the public highways and roads, in, over, or across the said commons, of less width than forty feet, so as none of such public roads shall be set out less than thirty feet".

We are going to focus on Liscard Common in particular because later this is where the main early growth of New Brighton as a sea-side resort together with the development of roads such as Rowson Street, Victoria Road and Warren Drive. This is in marked contrast to the prophecy contained in the above quotation.

The Commissioner's Award in 1812, after fixing the boundaries of the Township, sets out the position, length and boundaries of the public and private roads. The six public roads were the present Liscard Road, Martins Lane, part of Mill Lane, part of Wallasey Road, Magazine Lane and Mount Pleasant Road. and a short road of some eighty-six yards joining "the ancient road (Rake Lane) leading past William From's house to Liscard Common", with Magazine Lane. In addition, eleven private roads were built, including two main roads, Mount Road and part of Rowson Street.

Allocation was next made of the sites to be left open for the purpose of getting stone or marl for the use of the lord and land-holders in the Township namely :-

> Little Brighton Quarry (2 acres) - now the present Quarry Recreation Ground at the junction of Rowson Street and Magazine Lane

> Liscard Common Quarry (1 acre) - formerly the Quarry Gardens at the south-east corner of Tower Grounds

> Liscard Common, Marl Pit (1 acre) - now called the Captain's Pit, situated in Hose Side Road.

Land was then allotted to be sold to defray the expenses of the Act, made up of the following areas :-

> Lands comprising 44 acres of Liscard Moor, situated between Serpentine Road and Central Park Avenue on which Central Park and the ambulance station now stand, sold to Sir John Tobin.

> Lands comprising 25 acres of Liscard Common, now Vale Park, sold to John Penkett, Esquire, 'and by him sold to Thomas Twemlow and Samuel McDowall'

A small area of land approximately 2 roods and 2 perches in Liscard Common and partially enclosed by land recently purchased by John Penkett, sold to Samuel McDowall.

Six acres of land of the north west part of Liscard Common, formerly Stonebark (Warren Drive), sold to Sir John Tobin.

All the remaining common and waste lands in its two areas, Liscard Moor and Liscard Common, were then allocated to the various tenants of the Township, in right of their ancient enclosed lands.

Names well-known in the history of Wallasey and Liverpool appear including John Penkett, Sir John Tobin, James Mainwaring, Rev. Sir Henry Poole, John Deane, Thomas Molyneux, Sir John Grey Egerton, Robert Vyner, Sir. T. Stanely-Massey-Stanley and many others. Outstanding among these people in respect to the size of their allotments and purchases were the following :-

John Penkett, Esquire, Lord of the Manor who obtained a very large part of Liscard Common totaling some 187 acres of which 25 acres were sold to Thomas Twemlow and Samuel McDowall;

Sir John Tobin, whose holdings included a large part of Liscard Moor, approximately 50 acres together with some 24 acres in the north west corner of Liscard Common;

James Mainwaring, who was allotted 14 acres of Liscard Common and about 3 acres in Liscard Moor;

Samuel McDowall, who lands totalled some 35 acres of Liscard Common adjoining Magazine Lane. Apart from 2 roods 2 perches bordering his home which was allotted to him by the Commissioner, all his lands were purchased from the original holders namely. Thomas Deane, the Corporation of Liverpool, and John Penkett, Esquire;

Gerard Stanley, some 14 acres of Liscard Common;

Rev. Sir Henry Poole, some 13 acres of Liscard Common;

Sarah Strong, who obtained an area of approximately 12 acres of Liscard Common and a small holding of 1 rood 29 perches in Liscard Moor;

Members of the **Deane** Family:

John Deane, Senior (Deceased), approximately 5 acres of Liscard Common and 3 nearly 3 acres of Liscard Moor;

John Deane (Junior), some 6½ acres of Liscard Common and 1 acre in Liscard Moor;

Daniel Deane (Deceased), some 2 acres of Liscard Common and 1½ acres of Liscard Moor;

Sir John Grey Egerton, Bart, some 6 acres of Liscard Common;

Thomas Molyneux, some 4½ acres of Liscard Moor;

The Reverend George Briggs, Rector of Wallasey, was allotted a small holding of 1 rood 23 perches in Liscard Common and in connection with the Liscard Enclosures the following deed was drawn up in September, 1812:-

> Our Rector, the Rev. Geo. Briggs, being of opinion that he is entitled to immediate title of the late Liscard Enclosure and we the undersigned freeholders and tenants being of a contrary opinion do hereby agree (in order to maintain that good fellowship that has invariably existed amongst us) to allow our worthy Rector by way of compromise for the first six years commencing with the present crop and to be paid on or before the 1st day of December each year at and after the rate of seven shillings per year for every Cheshire acre we each of us shall plough or break up and continue the same even though any part that is once ploughed up should be converted to pasture.
>
> "And it is further agreed that should any new incumbent take possession of the living previous to the expiration of the said six years that we shall continue to pay him the above rate, but it is not to his wishes. Taking also into consideration the infirm state of health in which Mr Briggs is, we agree to appoint with his approbation Mr John Penkett and Sir John Tobin to collect the fore-mentioned rates and for them to pay over the same together with their own proportions to the Rector without giving him any trouble".
>
> Thomas Twemlow
> John Penkett
> Sam Dow
> Liscard, 1st Sept. 1812

The 1814 Act, entitled "An Act for Enclosing Lands in the Parishes of Wallasey and West Kirby, in the County of Chester", was much more comprehensive than that of 1809. The preamble was of the same legal terminology the substance being that there were in the Parishes of Wallasey commons and waste lands containing 640 acres in the Wallasey Leasowe and Wallasey Brake or Breck, exclusive of certain land covered with sand-hills on the North and North West side of the Wallasey Leasowe, and that there was also a certain tract or parcel of open land in the said township of Wallasey called Wallasey Pasture, containing about 220 acres, and in the township of Poulton-cum-Seacombe, Seacombe Dale, Hooks Common, and Poulton Common. As in the 1809 Act, James Boydell of Rossett, was appointed Commissioner, with "power" to set out and make such roads, ditches, drains, watercourses, bridges, walls, banks, tunnels, gates, stiles and other works ...as she shall think proper and convenient, useful, or necessary for the improvement of the Enclosed lands. Section 23 of the Act is worthy of special notice in view of the controversy following upon the action of the Corporation of Wallasey in railing-off the sand-hills in post-War years. It reads as follows :-

> "And be it further enacted, that nothing herein contained shall be construed to authorise the said Commissioner to divide, set out, or allot any of the land covered with sand hills, on the north-west side of the said commons or waste lands, in the township of Wallasey aforesaid, beyond such line or extent of land as the Commissioner may think for cultivation, but that the said sand hills shall remain unenclosed and open, for the better security and preservation of the land to the eastward and southward of the same, from the encroachments of the sea , and for which purpose such land covered with sand hills is hereby appropriated".

Under the Wallasey Improvement Act, 1845, the sand hills were placed under the control of the Wallasey Commissioners "but for no other use, intent or purpose whatsoever" than most that mentioned in the 1814 Act. This Act however, goes on to say "it shall be lawful for the said Commissioners to plant star grass, and to prevent trespass and damage thereon, and to take such other ways and means as in their judgment may be proper and necessary for the protection, care, and due preservation of the same."

The 1814 Act concludes by stating that nothing in the Act is in any way to "prejudice the right, title, or interest of the Lord or Lords of the said manors of Wallasey, and Poulton-cum-Seacombe, or of the said Richard Smith in respect of his ancient ferry of Seacombe."

The first section of the Commissioner's Award in reference to Wallasey, Leasowe, Wallasey Pasture, and Wallasey Brake deals with the setting out of the public and private roads. The roads that were fixed under the Act were Wallasey Village, Grove Road, Leasowe Road extending from Wallasey Village to Reeds Lane (the stone for building Leasowe Road came from Wallasey Breck), Breck Road, part of Claremount Road, Hose Side Road, Church Hill, Sandy Lane, Green Lane, Seaview Road and Sea Road. Worthy of note is the road from St. Hilary Brow to the Breck was cut through the rock by the contractor.

The Award then deals with the drainage of Wallasey Pasture, a low-lying and irregularly drained area adjoining the River Fender which flowed into the Wallasey Pool. Four public drains were fixed in connection with which a rate was drawn up apportioning the shares of the expenses of cleaning and maintaining the drains to the proprietors of Wallasey Pasture. The largest of these drains ran in an 'easterly direction along the north side of the Ancient fence dividing... the Wallasey Pasture from the Wallasey Leasowe." The remaining three ran southwards (from the first drain) and ultimately drained into the Fender running from Newton Carr to Wallasey Pool.

Provision, as in the 1809 Act, was made for the obtaining of marl and stone for the use of the lords and landowners but, in addition, the watering places were allotted for "the use and enjoyment of the inhabitants of the township of Wallasey", namely :-

1a Marl Pit (approx. 2 acres) - on the south side of Grove Road, opposite Sandcliffe Road;
2a The Brake or Breck Quarry (2 acres) - on the east side of Breck

Road but a road was to be left to Wallasey School;
Watering Pit (2 roods) at Springvale (Harrison Drive);
Watering Pit in the Little Wallacres, in 'the gather' (School Lane), a substitution for a public pit used by the inhabitants of Wallasey on Wallasey Breck enclosed in an allotment to Sir John Tobin.

Before proceeding to the general allotment of lands according to the rights of the land-holders the following areas were sold to defray the costs of the passing of the Act and its execution :-

Lands comprising approximately 16½ acres of Wallasey Leasowe, sold to the Rev. James Smedley;
Lands comprising some 47 acres of Wallasey Leasowe, sold to John Davies;
1 acre of Wallasey Leasowe, sold to William Peer;
20 perches of lands of Wallasey Leasowe, sold to Elizabeth Ashbrook;
Lands approximately 6 acres of Wallasey Leasowe, sold to Leigh Blundell, Esquire;
Lands approximately some 23 acres of Wallasey Leasowe bordering Leasowe Castle, sold to Mrs Boode, owner of the Castle;
About ½ acre of Wallasey Breck, sold to Henry Johnston;
A very large area, nearly some 260 acres, of Wallasey Leasowe bordered on the north by the land covered by with sand hills left unenclosed by the Award, sold to the Rev. Augustus Cambell, Rector of Wallasey;
1½ acres of Wallasey Leasowe, sold to George Peers;
Containing 3 acres of Wallasey Pasture, sold to Thomas Sparks.

The remaining lands of Wallasey Leasowe, Wallasey Breck, and Wallasey Pasture, were then allotted to the land-holders of the township according to their rights of commons and "cowgaits" (or "Pasture Gate" which was a right to turn out to the common, a certain number of horses, cows, sheep or goats) in respect of their ancient enclosed lands. The chief recipients of land, either by allotment or purchase, in the township enclosures were the following :-

Robert Vyner, Esquire - one of the Lords of the Manor, who obtained a large share of the western part of Wallasey Leasowe, together with certain areas in the Wallasey Pasture and Wallasey Breck; the whole totalling some 63 acres of Wallasey Leasowe, 34 acres of Wallasey Pasture and 13 perches in Wallasey Brake.

Sir John Grey Egerton, Bart. - the other Lord of the Manor, who likewise was allotted lands in each of the areas made up as follows. 34½ acres of Wallasey Leasowe, 20½ acres of Wallasey Pasture, and approximately 2 acres of Wallasey Breck.

Sir John Tobin, Knight - whose holdings included about 44 acres of Wallasey Leasowe, 43½ acres of Wallasey Pasture, together with 6½ acres of Wallasey Breck.

Mr John Davies - who at the time of the Award, obtained some 37 acres of Wallasey Leasowe, and 4½ acres of Wallasey Pasture. In addition, it is very probable that Mr John Davies acquired the very large holding of about 260 acres in Wallasey Leasowe, sold by the Commissioner to the Rev. Augustus Campbell. There is no indication of this in the Award but in the 1846 Map of Wallasey made from surveys for the commutation of the Tithes in 1841, this area is shown as having been purchased by the Rev. Augustus Campbell on behalf of John Davies, Esquire.

John Leigh, Esquire - who share of Wallasey Leasowe was 23½ acres.

Mrs. Margaret Boode - owner of Leasowe Castle, who purchased approximately 23 acres of Wallasey Leasowe adjoining the Castle.

The Rev. Augustus Campbell - Rector of Wallasey (1814-1825), succeeding the late Rev. George Briggs in 1814, who in addition to the purchase of land on behalf of John Davies also obtained, as Rector of Wallasey Church, the Glebe Lands, which comprised of some 7 acres of Wallasey Leasowe and 34 perches of Wallasey Breck;

Robert Harrison - whose acquisitions of land comprised some 11 acres of the extreme westerly part of Wallasey Leasowe;

Rev James Smedley - who, by purchase, obtained about 16½ acres of Wallasey Leasowe;

Joseph Green - whose holdings included 14 acres of Wallasey Leasowe together with 12 acres of Wallasey Pasture;

Richard Smith, Esquire, Lord of the Manor of Poulton-cum-Seacombe - who obtained small areas in each of the open lands, namely, 3½ acres of Wallasey Leasowe, 4 acres of Wallasey Pasture and 1 acre of Wallasey Breck.

In addition to the foregoing people, many others received smaller holdings among whom were George and William Peers, members of the Deane family descendants of whom remained prominent market-gardeners for many years, the trustees of Matthew Taylor, Thomas Molyneux, Peter Ledsham, heirs if Elizabeth Bird, Sir T. Massey-Stanley-Massey Bart., the devisees in trust of the Rev. George Briggs, the late Rector of Wallasey), and Thomas Sparks.

The Award then proceeds to deal with the allocation of the 91 acres of common and waste lands in the Township of Poulton-cum-Seacombe Dale, Hooks Common and Poulton Common. Four public roads were fixed now represented by the important highways of Borough Road, starting at the Old Seacombe Ferry House, the northern end of Whiteling's Lane (known today as Wheatland Lane), Poulton Bridge Road, and part of Breck Road.

Some of the several private roads set out have become of any importance. After selling a few small areas of land (lands which formed the eastern part if Seacombe Common, bordering the River Mersey), the main allocations of territory were established the greater part of which went to the following people :-

Richard Smith, Esquire, Lord of the Manor whose lands comprised about 12 acres of Seacombe Common, some 2 acres of Seacombe Dale, and about 18½ acres Hook's Common, together with two very small allocations in Mill Lane approximating to about ½ acre;

James Mainwaring, Esquire, who obtained 7½ acres of Seacombe Common, 8 acres of Hook's Common, and like Richard Smith, two very small holdings in Mill Lane;

Robert Vyner, Esquire, Lord of the Manor of Wallasey, who obtained about half the total area of Poulton Common (some 2 acres) and about 3 acres of Hook's Common;

Sir John Tobin whose allocations were limited to three small areas, one of about ½ acre in Seacombe Common, another 1½ acres of Hook's Common, and the third of only 8 perches in Mill Lane.

The Trustees of Wallasey School, who were allotted 1 acre of Seacombe Common, 1½ acres of Hook's Common, and a very small holding of only 15 perches in Mill Lane.

Other small allotments went to Samuel Smith, Thomas Molyneux, William Pendleton, Leigh Blundell Esq., Thomas Lowry and William Bird (of Bird House, Poulton).

The Wallasey Ship Canal

Although the Act for enclosing the waste lands and commons in the townships of Wallasey and Poulton-cum-Seacombe was passed in 1814, the actual Award of the Commissioner only took place in May 1823.

Meanwhile, the interest of Sir John Tobin, one of the chief landholders in Wallasey, had been awakened to the possibilities of a ship canal through Wallasey Pool and across the marshlands of North Wirral to the mouth of the River Dee and he in conjunction with William Laird (the pioneer of shipbuilding on Merseyside) and others, obtained expert advice from the engineers Thomas Telford, Robert Stevenson, and Alexander Nimmo.

A comprehensive and ambitious report was given by these in 1828, with details regarding the deepening and widening of Wallasey Pool and the construction of docks and tidal basins with warehouse accommodation; these docks were to be linked with further dock facilities at Hilbre Island by a "canal proceeding at first in the direction of Leasowe Lighthouse, and approaching within half-a-mile of the shore, and about the same distance north of the village of Moreton, and then turning to the westwards, keeping half-a-mile inland from the villages of Great and Little Meols through Newton Carr where it turns off Hilbre Island.

The estimated cost of all these works was given at £1,400,948 for which "a floating harbour will be obtained of seven miles in length, capable of indefinite enlargement, with extensive warehouse accommodation, and with a seaport at either end on the two separate estuaries". The advantage to be obtained from this scheme was :-

1. Additional dock areas with land available for warehouses and industrial activities, the Liverpool docks being inadequate to the growing needs of Merseyside;

2. Vessels entering the canal at or near Dawpool would pay dues to the Port of Chester and thus escape the heavier dock and town dues of Liverpool;

3. Avoidance of the difficult Mersey Channels especially the Rock Channels, at that time the main passage to and from the harbour of Liverpool.

These works, if they had been carried out, would very probably have modified the history of Wallasey during the nineteenth century and given its growth a more-marked industrial character.

When, however, time came to apply for parliamentary sanction it was revealed that a large part of the land adjoining Wallasey Pool had been purchased privately by the Corporation of Liverpool. Accordingly, the undertaking was abandoned and North Wirral was allowed to retain its rural character.

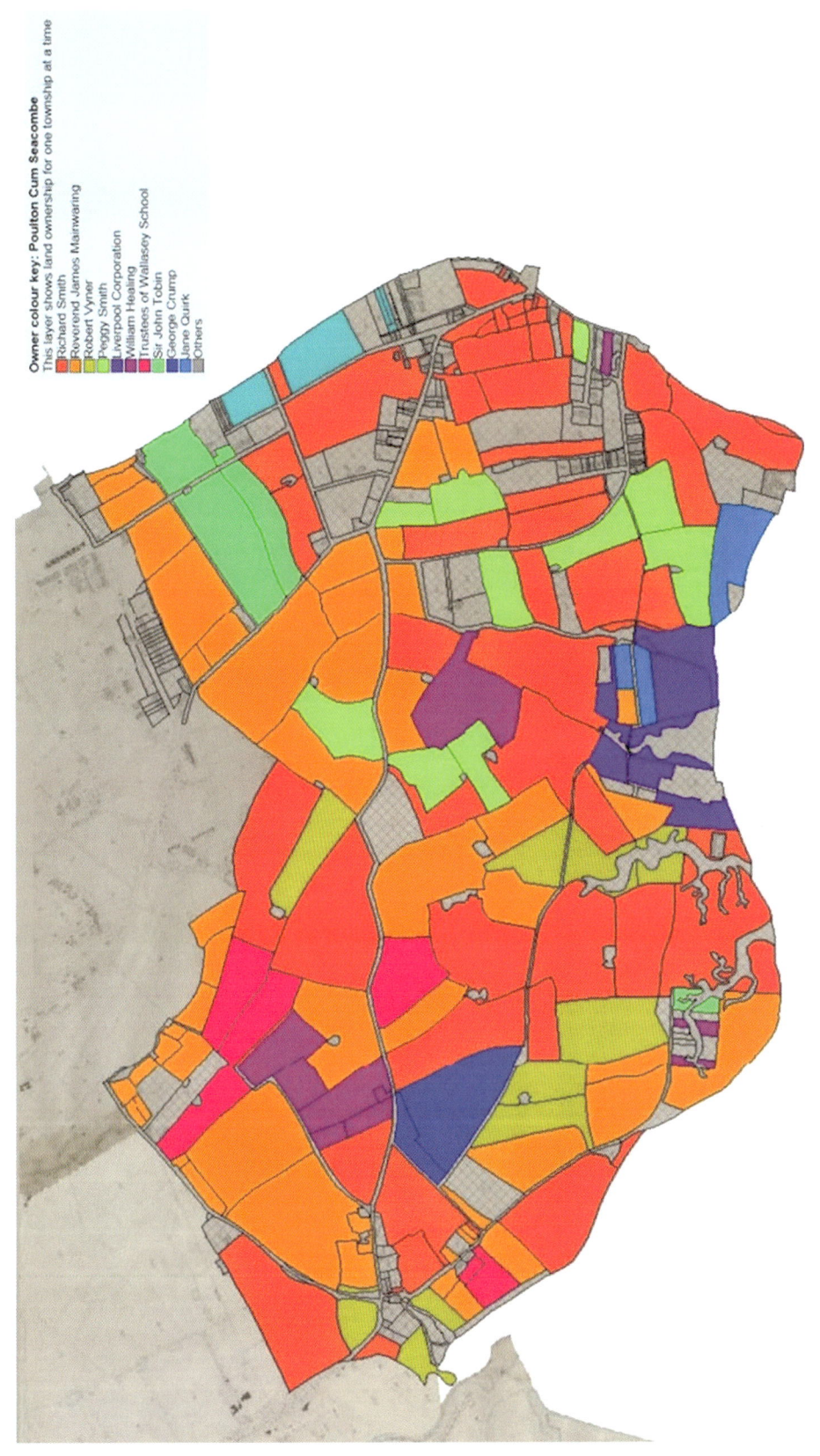

Tithe Map, 1841, showing landowners of Poulton-cum-Seacombe

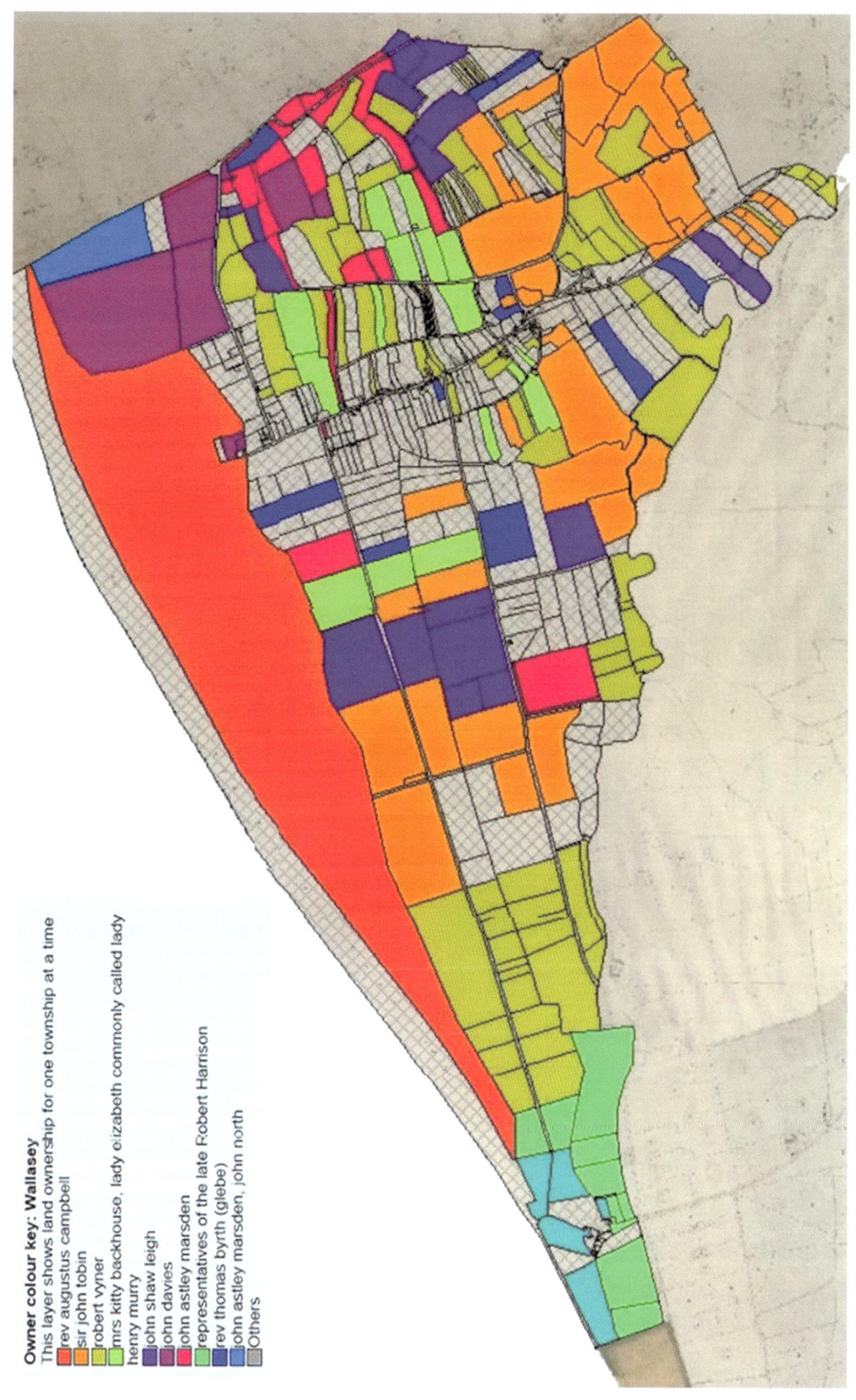

Tithe Map, 1841, showing landowners of Wallasey Village

Chapter 3

Wallasey From 1831 – 1851

Before considering the development in Wallasey between 1831 to 1851 it is worth just studying briefly the conditions of the Wirral as a whole in 1831. The population density of the Wirral Township had changed rapidly in 1801 and 1831 which resulted in a change in the distribution of the population. In general, the greater part of the Wirral in 1831 had retained its agricultural character with a scanty population. Neston and Parkgate had a very slight increase and still maintained its dominance in the western or Deeside portion but in contrast it had lost its outstanding importance in the Wirral as a whole. The north-east corner comprising Birkenhead and Wallasey was easily the most densely peopled area. Here, the densities in the townships passing from north to south had increased as follows :-

	1801	1831
	person per 100 acres	
Liscard	23	107
Poulton-cum-Seacombe	21	146
Birkenhead	12	287
Tranmere	33	109

The main reason for these increases is to be found in the growth of Liverpool and the beginning of the absorption of the Merseyside part of the Wirral into its sphere of influence, which was to become more and more pronounced as the century advanced. This resulted largely from the development of better and safer ferry services across the river and in connection with this second important factor was becoming more evident in the case of Birkenhead. This factor was the growth of better land communications especially in regard to coach services on the Birkenhead-Chester Road and the through route to Liverpool to London, via Birkenhead and Chester. Wallasey, however, in regard to land communications still remained largely isolated.

Growth of Population In Wallasey, 1831-1851

Year	Wallasey Township	Liscard Township	Poulton-cum-Seacombe	Parish of Wallasey
1801	274	211	178	663
1811	440	289	214	943
1821	444	345	380	1169
1831	558	967	1212	2737
1841	942	2872	2446	6261
1851	1195	4100	3044	8339

The figures shown above from the Census Reports illustrate clearly the changes in Wallasey to which reference has already been made. Up to 1831 there had been a certain amount of increase, from 663 to 2737, which was felt mainly in the Townships of Poulton-cum-Seacombe and Liscard, but it is in the next decade that the increase becomes most marked. In contrast to the increase of 2064 in the first 30 years of the century the next two decades show an increase 3524 and 2078 respectively. The main increases were in the two Townships bordering the Mersey and Wallasey Township showed a much lower increase. In this period then there is the beginning of the growth of modern Wallasey and its emergence from the almost mediaeval conditions that prevailed at the beginning of the century.

The chief reasons for this remarkable increase in population can be summarised as follows :-

a. The attraction of the area as a residential district in close proximity to Liverpool;
b. The establishment of new and better ferries;
c. The development of New Brighton as a sea-side resort;
d. The establishment of docks and attendant industries in the southern part of the region, bordering Wallasey Pool.

These factors are almost identical with those accounting for the even more marked growth of Birkenhead in the same period (1831: 2,569, 1841: 8,223, 1851: 24,285).

(a) The attraction of Wallasey as a residential area in close proximity to Liverpool was very strong. Liverpool, in the immediate vicinity of the docks and commercial centre, was becoming overcrowded and people were being forced further afield. Consequently, Wallasey with its open, rural character and sea-side position appealed strongly to the Liverpool merchants. Until about 1830, however, the absence of adequate ferry facilities for crossing the river had made it well-nigh impossible for those wishes to be gratified. After that date the position was radically changed.

(b) The Growth of The Ferries. At the beginning of the century the only ferry of any importance was the primitive one with its small sailing or rowing boats in Seacombe. Probably another existed between Liverpool and the Magazines but this would almost wholly be used by those who had business with the ships laying off the Magazines in the "Gutter" (in a Liverpool Directory of 1821 states that sail boats were constantly plying between Liverpool and the Magazines. This persisted in diminishing importance until about 1846).

Seacombe Ferry. The 1814 Enclosure Act, refers to the rights of Richard Smith as Lord of the Manor of Poulton-cum-Seacombe in respect of his ancient ferry at Seacombe. Following upon litigation in 1816-1817 between Richard Smith and the Rev. James Mainwaring over this ferry which was settled in favour of the former, he leased it to Thomas Parry who ran it in connection with Parry's Seacombe Hotel, a popular place of entertainment and refreshment which 'obtained a high reputation among its numerous visitors, and the gourmands of Liverpool.' Even so, its influence as a factor in the development of residential Wallasey was very limited as long as sailing vessels were in use with their slow and irregular services dependent largely upon the weather. In 1829, however, steam boats were plying every hour from Liverpool and the scene was set for further improvements in 1835 when a new stone pier was constructed by Mr Parry, and a few years later (prior to 1843) when a new floating landing stage was placed in position.

Seacombe Ferry, 1830

Early view of New Brighton Pier, c1860

In 1843 the fare across was three-pence. Meanwhile, new ferries had been established, again by private enterprise, at Egremont and New Brighton.

Egremont Ferry. Mention has already been made of the dispute in 1816-1817 between Richard Smith and James Mainwaring over Seacombe Ferry. Apparently, a little later a further dispute arose between Mr Parry and Sir John Tobin who had by this time purchased a share in the Manor of Wallasey. It is very probable that from this quarrel resulted the establishment of Egremont Ferry at the southern limit of Liscard Township by the joint efforts of Sir John Tobin and Captain John Askew in 1829-30. The latter gentleman coming from Cumbria named his house 'Egremont' after his native town, and gradually the settlement that grew up around his house and ferry acquired a similar name. As at Seacombe, a fashionable hotel was established in connection with the Ferry. Subsequently, various changes in ownership took place until 1850 when both Egremont and New Brighton Ferries were owned by Mr Edward Warburton Coulbourn who managed them until 1861, when both Ferries were purchased by the Wallasey Local Board under the Improvement Acts of 1845, 1858 and 1861.

New Brighton Ferry. In the meantime further private enterprise had resulted in the construction of New Brighton Ferry in relation to the development of the northern part of Liscard Township as a fashionable sea-side resort. It will be remembered that the Enclosure Award of 1823 had resulted in the division of Liscard Common to a number of plots of land of which the greater part had gone to John Penkett, Lord of Liscard Manor. This land in turn was sold in 1830, to James Atherton, a retired Liverpool merchant interested in building and land speculation, together with part of the land allotted to Sarah Strong. All these lands, totalling approximately 163 acres appear, according to the 1841 Map of Wallasey, to have been shared by James Atherton and his son-in-law, William Rowson of Prescot.

Together they planned to lay out this expense of heathland and sandhills as the future watering place of the north of England, to be called New

Brighton in distinction to the older established sea-side resort of the South Coast. The attractions of the future New Brighton were set forth convincingly in the following prospectus which reads in part somewhat similarly to the growing descriptions of many of mid-20th Century Sea-Side Resort Illustrated Guides.

'As New Brighton is likely to become a favourite and fashionable Watering Place, several Gentlemen have proposed to erect there a handsome hotel, and a convenient Dock and Ferry to be called 'The Royal Light House Hotel and Ferry' and to establish a communication by Stena Packets between that place and Liverpool.

The expense of this undertaking is established at £12,000, and it is intended to raise this sum in shares of £100 such, to be placed under the management of a Committees to be chosen annually or otherwise by the subscribers.

To persons inclined to take shares this will be an eligible investment, as it holds out a prospect of an annual return of at least 20 per cent, an expectation well-grounded upon its many and various advantages.

New Brighton is situated at the Rock Point, three miles division from Liverpool, and from its elevated situation commands from all points the most interesting and extensive views. The Welch Mountains, the Orme's heads and the Isle of Man are all distinctly visible, whilst its more immediate prospect embraces the opposite shares of Crosby and Bootle, the Docks and Port of Liverpool, and the furtile County of Chester.

As a Bathing Place it has peculiar advantages not only from its being the nearest point to the open sea, but it also possesses the most beautiful beach.

The sands are hard and clean, free from and, gravel or quicksands, they are many miles in extent and cannot be equalled for the purpose of exercise, whether in carriages, on foot, or on horseback.

As the tide never recedes more than 200 yards from the land, it prevents those disagreeable exhalations so common on other shores, whilst it renders bathing safe and practicable at all hours. New Brighton also possesses a more interesting sea view than any other watering place can boast, being constantly enlivened by the passaging of vessels to and from the rich and flourishing Port of Liverpool, in many instances approaching so near as to admit of persons on the shore conversing with those on board.

The proprietors intend to avail themselves of the natural advantages afforded by the undulations of the ground to erect all villas on such sites that one shall not intercept the view of another, but that all shall enjoy the same beauty and extent of prospect. Among its other advantages may be enumerated the salubrity of the air, the certain supply of purest spring water, the aspect of all the rooms fronting the sea, enjoying the refreshing breeze, and sheltered from the oppressive heat of the afternoon's sun, while its proximity to Liverpool, together with the certainty and safety of the Steam Navigation must lend to render New Brighton a most agreeable and desirable place of resort to the Nobility and Gentry of all the neighbouring Counties.

It is intended to erect a Church, Market Place, Shops and Buildings that will include a Reading Room, Baths, Billiard Room, Post Office, etc, etc, and indeed nothing will be left undone to make it a most attractive and fashionable Watering Place.

Under such circumstances the Hotel and Ferry must combine great advantages, strangers will prefer stopping here, as they can at once step into any Packet without any inconvenience, and the Steam of Vessels or affording assistance to ships in distress.

The Grounds are now laying out in such a manner as it is hoped will command admiration. The public are referred to the Plans, and invited to view the different sites for buildings, and if New Brighton is in their opinion deserving of their patronage, the Proprietors will offer the land for Villas at a price worthy of their attention. Applications for purchase of land to be made to James Atherton, Esq., New Brighton, or to Mr Rowson, Prescot'.

(date October 1832)

William Rowson

William Rowson was born in Prescot, Lancashire in 1791. He was the fourth of five children born to Henry and Martha Rowson (nee Higson), who were married at Prescot in 1786. William's father, Henry, (1763-1825), was an attorney by profession, and, significantly, was the elder brother of Betty Rowson, James Atherton's future wife. William trained in his father's profession, and in 1818 he married James and Betty's eldest daughter, Mary, his first cousin; an event not uncommon in early nineteenth century England, particularly among wealthier class, who almost exclusively, married within their own class.

From a practical point of view, James Atherton could not have wished for a better suited and qualified ally. Here was a man trained in the law, who was wealthy, young and ambitious, and what is more, a member of the family; who better to take over the reins of control - bearing in mind additionally that Atherton had recently lost three of his sons. Perhaps William Rowson lacked the flair of his father-in-law, but he did appear to possess the necessary business acumen to become, at least potentially, as successful as Atherton had been when he developed Everton Village in the 1800's. It is quite conceivable that James Atherton fully recognised this potential and acted accordingly.

William and Mary Rowson, who never had any children, appear to move into 'Cliff Villa', Wellington Road, in the autumn of 1833, where they remained until William died in February 1863 at the age of 72 and Betty died shortly afterwards, aged 70, in September 1864. Both were laid to rest in the graveyard of the Parish Church of St. Hilary in Wallasey Village.

Following upon this prospectus and scheme a wooden pier was erected with a cafe at the shore and a small run out stage on lines at the river end. This wooden structure lasted until 1867 when the first floating stage and iron pier supplanted it. The ferry itself was very primitive with small, paddle steam-boats plying supplemented apparently as late as 1840 by rowing boats by a single sail. The ferry also was open only during the summer closing in October when the boats were laid up for the winter. Even so the ferry was exceedingly important in the development of New Brighton both as a residential area and a sea-side resort.

(c) The Development of New Brighton as a Sea-Side Resort. The beginnings of New Brighton have already been indicated in reference to the building of the Ferry and the proposed laying-out of this shore. Gradually they became the haunt of a very troublesome class of people and the place for a short time had a very disreputable character. It was called 'The Nest' but by some 'The Devils Nest'.

(d) The Industrial Development of Southern Wallasey bordering the Pool. Following upon the abortive scheme of Tobin and William Laird (1828) for the construction of docks on Wallasey Pool and a canal joining these with Hilbre on the Dee, several industries were established on both sides of the Pool. In 1824, Laird had set up a boiler manufactory, situated at the foot of Livingstone Street in Birkenhead, to which a ship-building yard was soon added. After 1828, the firm of William Laird and Son turned their attention principally to ship-building and the use of iron instead of wood, became the pioneers in iron ship-building and constructed prior to 1840 some 32 iron vessels of all kinds.

Meanwhile, the increased prosperity of Birkenhead and the readiness of Liverpool corporation to dispose of their land holdings adjoining the Pool led to the revival of the Dock Scheme, In 1843, Mr Laird bought 48,000 square yards at Wallasey Pool which paved the way for the purchase in all of some 200,000 square yards by him and others from the Corporation of Liverpool. Acts of Parliament were passed in 1844 and 1845 and work was begun by which the Pool was to be turned into a vast systems of Docks, the provision of which would have given a great impetus to the growth of Wallasey and Birkenhead as well as to the whole of Merseyside. The study of the Dock construction is too long to be dealt with fully but it should be noted that in 1846, reaction set in and although 1847 saw in April the opening of the Morpeth and Egerton Docks, it also saw the tremendous decline in Birkenhead's population from about 40,000 in January to 20,000 in December. The reason for this partial failure of the Dock Scheme are to be found in :-

(1) the unsatisfactory finances of the Birkenhead Commissioners;

(2) the work itself although well planned was badly carried out;

(3) Liverpool Corporation not only gave no support to the scheme but did everything possible to impede its progress.

The Commissioners attempted unsuccessfully to carry on the Dock scheme but in 1855, they passed under the control of the Corporation of Liverpool and then, in 1857, under that, of the Mersey Docks and Harbour Board.

In the meantime, favoured by the water facilities a number of industries had been established on the Wallasey side of the Pool including the following which appeared on tithe maps of c1841 :-

(a) Copper Works of Messrs John Bibby, Sons and Company near Creek Side, off Dock Road;
(b) Smalt Works of Dawdsley and Smith
(c) Seacombe Foundry of Messrs Pollard and Co., to the north-west of the Smalt Works
(d) Starch and Vitriol Works of Messrs Clough and Galan, just west of the Copper Works.

A little later than 1846 other industries came into existence which included :-

(e) Seacombe Pottery, which stood on the land which was partly occupied by Messrs. Currie and Rowland's works. This was built in 1851, by Mr. Goodwin of Staffordshire and at the time was supposed to be the best built and equipped pottery in England. It produced earthenware and stoneware, chiefly of a blue colour, as well as colour ware and colour-printed ware. Later, Parian ware was made in large quantities;

(f) Sugar Refinery, which stood close to the pottery;

(g) Cement Works of Mr. George F. Chantrell of Leeds, established about 1855 a little north of the Copper Works;

(h) Phospho Peruvian Guano Works was situated in Havelock Street (later renamed Alfred Road) which commenced about 1830. In addition there were the Linke-kilns, shown on Eye's Survey of 1839, standing at the end of Limekiln Lane, near the edge of the Pool, but not appearing on the 1841 map.

Distribution of Land-Holders and Settlements in 1846

The combined influence of all these factors is clearly seen in a study of the settlements shown on the 1841-46 Map of Wallasey (Wallasey Village, Poulton-cum-Seacombe, Liscard, Egremont, New Brighton). This reveals that several new hamlets had come into existence since 1811, all of which were in the eastern part of the Parish, the part bordering the river and thus they were in close proximity to the three ferries with their facilities for reaching Liverpool. Here land speculation for building purpose had already begun and plots of land had been purchased from the old land-holders and their descendants. Apart from these purchases of land near the ferries and in New Brighton the land-holdings were much the same as in the earlier part of the century.

In Liscard Township the Manor had passed to John Dencil Maddock, the grandson of Thomas Maddock, Rector of Liverpool 1772-1782, who had married his first cousin Mary Anne Penkett, daughter of the late Lord of the Manor, John Penkett. His holdings formed a fairly compact block of land lying to the north, south and west of Liscard Manor House (bottom of Manor Lane). To the north-west were the lands purchased by John Astley Marsden, a brush manufacturer of Liverpool. These encircled the so-called Liscard Castle, which stood a little back from the northern end of Marsden Lane (now Seaview Road). It was a large and stately house but its battlements and stone lion embellishments resulted in it being called ironically 'Brush Castle' and later 'Liscard Castle'. Later in the century the house was divided into three parts, the Turrets, the Towers and the Castle. Following upon their demolition roads were built on the site and named accordingly. In the south-west of the Township the lands of Sir John Tobin had passed by marriage and purchased to Harold Littledale, Esquire. The latter was a Cumberland gentleman, head of a great mercantile house in Liverpool (he was Mayor of Liverpool in 1827), and had married Margaret, daughter of Sir John Tobin, joint holder of the Manor of Wallasey with Robert Vyner, Esq. His lands in Liscard occupied a large part of the Old Moor, lying on either side of Liscard Road. About the centre was 'Moor Hey House', afterwards called Liscard Hall. This fine house had been built by Sir John Tobin about 1835. Just outside the Township boundary, bordering Mill Lane, was Littledale's Model Farm which until about 1870 was one of the few big sources of employment in Wallasey. This farm was an expensive hobby of Littledale and contained some 40 acres, including much of the best arable and pasture land in the whole Parish.

The steward's house and the milk and cheese house was where the dairy maids lived, still stand in Rullerton Road. Some of the cottages (with diamond pane windows) occupied by the farm hands once stood opposite the old maternity home in Mill Lane. The shippons and stables stood further inside, abreast of the cottages. For some reason the shippons never numbered more than 99 in three shippons. The piggeries near the end of Marlowe Road, and the great corn and hay stacks, with the farm buildings, stood on the north side of the shippons. The sheep farm was on the Wallasey golf-links land, the shepperd's house being at the junction of Green Lane with the path leading from Leasowe Road over the sandhills to the shore. The cows were all stall-fed, and many people believed the milk to be unwholesome on that account, but as Littledale's milk (and butter and cheese) was consumed all over Wallasey without any ill-effects being found, the story was probably untrue. Farmers came from all parts of the world to view the farm.

All the drainage from the shippons and stables drained into a large bank, which led by underground pipes to various fields, and the liquid was pumped over them after the crop had been cut, and several crops were thus collected each summer. The fields at the corner of Martin's Lane and where the ambulance station is now were noted for their wonderful grass and corn crops.

Many of the farm hands came annually from Ireland and North Wales to work in the summer. Some of them settled in Wallasey and their descendants are still to be found.

In the Township of Poulton-cum-Seacombe the land-holdings were mainly in the hands of Admiral Richard Smith and the Rev. James Mainwaring, joint proprietors of the Manor, with isolated areas owned by Robert Vyner, Esquire., including most of Poulton Common. Bordering the Pool were the sections of land purchased by the founders of the various industrial activities already mentioned, together with the holding of the Corporation of Liverpool.

In the Township of Wallasey the lands were still largely owned by Robert Vyner, Esquire, and Harold Littledale, joint-holders of the Manor, with fair-sized holdings controlled by John Shaw Leigh, Esquire, John Astley Marsden, and John Davies. There were also many smaller patches including those owned by members of the Deane family.

At this time, the middle of the nineteenth century, there were ten small settlements in contrast to the five at the beginning of the century. These were the original five: Wallasey Village, Poulton Village, Liscard Village, Seacombe Village and the small Magazines settlement together with the new ones of New Brighton, Upper or Little Brighton, North Egremont, Egremont, and Somerville.

New Brighton - The origin of this settlement has already been discussed in reference to Atherton and Rowson's scheme for the development of a sea-side resort. Building had followed and by now a number of houses and shops were in existence. These were mainly in the south side of Victoria Road and beginning from the ferry included the Ferry Hotel, a few shops at the bottom of Victoria Road, and the New Brighton Hotel, the row of houses (later shops) then St. George's Terrace (which extended from Grosvenor Road to Rowson Street). Beyond Rowson Street were a few houses reaching St. James' Church which was already in existence, and after a break came the large houses in Montpelier Crescent which were plastered with stucco and painted usually a buff colour, a style of house that of the nineteenth century. On the shore frontage moving round from the Ferry were the 'Nest' and a number of wooden erections used as shops for supplying hot water for tea to the summer visitors, then came the fine large houses on the sea-ward side of Wellington Road between Atherton Street and the Red Noses. Other small brick-built houses existed in a terrace-formation in Egerton Street.

Upper Brighton consisted of a few large houses along the eastern side of Upper Rowson Street together with a number of small, terrace-formation, brick houses that once stood immediately to the west of the Quarry Recreation Ground. The housing density map of Wallasey, 1935, showed this area was the second highest density in the whole of Wallasey, namely 64 houses per acre.

The Magazines had remained practically unchanged except for a few additions in the latter half of the nineteenth century. The outstanding additions included a further terrace formation of small houses in Beech Grove (at the bottom of Holland Road and Liscard Vale (now the house and cafe in Vale Park). Nearby, at the bottom of Magazine Lane stood Liscard Hotel which in 1857 was known as New Brighton Hotel, and still later as 'The Stanley Arms'. Finally, until largely destroyed by fire in 1854, it existed as 'New Brighton College' under the control of Dr. Poggi, a friend of Garibaldi whose two sons Riclotti and Menotti were educated there.

North Egremont lay further to the south between the newly constructed Manor Road (prior to 1841) and Trafalgar Road. It included a number of large houses on the new Seabank Road (joining Manor Road to the new roads King Street and Brighton Street that led through North Egremont and Egremont to Seacombe Ferry) and along Trafalgar Road. In addition, there were a number of smaller houses between what is now Stringhey Road and Poole Road.

Egremont as previously mentioned, had grown up behind John Askew's ferry and comprised a number of large houses laid out in connection with several newly constructed roads. Church Street was the chief road leading from the ferry approach westwards to St. John's Church which had been erected by Sir John Tobin. Other roads were Union Street and Burnaby Street, the latter forming a narrow street between the backs of the houses in Church Street.

Seacombe had developed considerably but most of the property was made up of small houses in the Mersey Street area (which were demolished in the 1930s as an unhealthy area and re-built with then Corporation Houses at a density of 18 houses per acre) and Demesne Street and Brighton Street. Better class houses existed along Victoria Road (now Borough Road). Church Road had been constructed leading from the Ferry to St. Paul's Church, the foundation stone of which was laid 6th June, 1846. The church was built during the succeeding year in the Early Middle Pointed Style of the 13th Century with a spire 120 feet high completed in 1849. To the south-west of the Church and extending on both sides of Wheatland Lane were the small houses built probably to accommodate the employees of the Phospho Peruvian Guenon Works in Havelock Street (now Alfred Road), and the other industrial works bordering the Pool.

Somerville, lying about mid-way between Poulton and Seacombe, consisted of about a dozen very fine, large houses fronting on the Poulton Road with a few smaller houses at the back facing the present Halstead Road. Almost mid-way between Somerville and Poulton, Gorsey Lane had been constructed leading south-west from Poulton Road to the Docks which were in construction at this time (1846).

Liscard Village, situated at some distance from any of the ferries had remained practically unchanged until the construction of two long terraces of small brick-built houses along the present St. Alban's Road and Terraces. These properties were possibly built for the people employed on Littledale's Model Farm (the houses remained until the 1960's until being demolished to make way for Dominic House and town centre car park). Also properties were built along Egerton Grove as well as half a dozen larger houses had been built along the western side of Marsden Lane (now Seaview Road) near where Fairview Avenue is today.

Poulton and Wallasey Village, likewise, showed little signs of development in regard to housing which was explained by their distance from the ferries.

The growth of population and the associated settlements resulted in the appointment in 1845 of Commissioners to undertake the paving, lighting, watching, cleansing and improvement of the Parish. Unfortunately, the Commissioners appointed almost wholly neglected their duties and sanitary conditions became so bad that in 1851 a considerable number of the inhabitants of Seacombe led by their Incumbent Rev. Edward Roberts, petitioned the General Board of Health to appoint an inspector to visit the locality and to report thereon. Subsequently, in the same year, an Enquiry was held at Parry's Hotel, Seacombe, by Mr. Robert Rawlinson, Superintendent Inspector under the Public Health Act. His report gives an interesting picture of the very unsatisfactory state of affairs in the Township of Poulton-cum-Seacombe. It revealed that there were no public lights in the parish, and only a small private gasworks which supplied Egremont Ferry, no public supply of water, and that the roads were very dirty, especially in winter. The housing conditions in the Mersey Street area, adjoining Seacombe Ferry were described as abominable and the mortality rate in Poulton-cum-Seacombe "was excessive and that with all the natural advantages of the locality, it was greater than even in the worst districts of Liverpool. The unsanitary conditions had partly arisen in the way described by the Seacombe petitioners as follows :-

> "We have to observe that all the drains and sewers from the houses and water-closets of the village of Seacombe deposit their filthy contents upon the shore, the stench from which is not only highly offensive to the senses but extremely prejudicial to health.
>
> That before a certain embankment was raised by the Trustees of the Birkenhead Docks, the tidal waters of the River Mersey washed the before-mentioned shore daily, and consequently removed all impurities; that the said tide is now excluded, and that a cesspool is formed within the said embankment, which engenders malaria, and will

in the coming hot season be a fruitful source of fever and diseases to a neighbourhood already notorious for its unhealthiness".

The Inspector also expressed the opinion that conditions in the Parish of Wallasey generally were similar to those in Poulton-cum-Seacombe. Inevitably, this report resulted in the displacement of the existing Commissioners and in 1853 a Local Board of Health was created under the Public Health Acts of 1848 and 1853. The progress of Wallasey under the Local Board of Health and its successors in public administration forms the subject matter as we continue the story of Wallasey into the second half of the nineteenth century.

Victoria Road (renamed later as Borough Road), 1879

The Wallasey Mill above the Breck, c1870

The Devil's Nest, c1865. Originally built for the workers of the fort but later occupied by undesirables, such as beachtraders and hawkers.

The burnt out shell of St. Hilary's Church which caught fire in 1857

Gorsey Lane, looking up towards Poulton Road, 1925

New Brighton Promenade, c1910, between Rowson Street and Waterloo Road

Chapter 4

Wallasey From 1851 to 1914

The second half of the 19th Century and the first few years of the 20th Century was a period that saw a truly remarkable growth of population and urbanistaion in Wallasey; a period also of consolidation when the fundamental role of Wallasey with its three-fold importance as a residential area, a sea-side resort, and an industrial town, became fully established. As the factors influencing this three-fold development in its incipient stages in the first half of the century has been covered in Wallasey 1831 to 1851 it is therefore the section is best dealt with as brief as possible.

Growth of Population 1851 – 1911

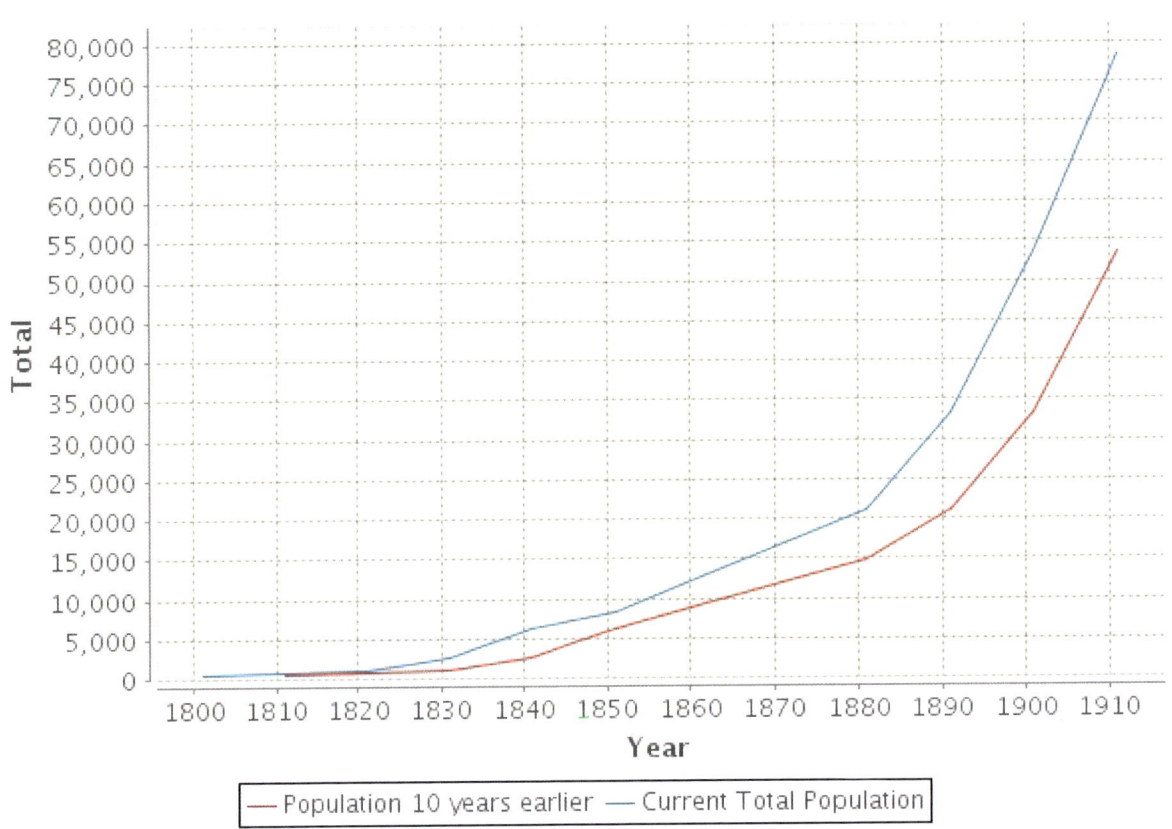

From the graph of population on the previous page it will be seen that the population of Wallasey increased with great rapidity from 8,329 in 1851 to

78,504 in 1911. This large growth was typical of the north-east corner of the Wirral owing mainly to its proximity to Liverpool.

In 1851, as throughout the century, the greater part of the Wirral retained its rural, agricultural character but in the north-eastern area, comprising Wallasey and Birkenhead, the population density was growing rapidly and the townships concerned were steadily being urbanised. The densities were as follows in 1851 and 1871 :-

	1851	1871
	person per 100 acres	
Liscard	456	697
Poulton-cum-Seacombe	376	607
Birkenhead	2693	3280
Tranmere	609	1510
Lower Bebington	142	359
Higher Bebington	157	346
Oxton	248	322
Claughton	166	569
Wallasey	75	122

The last five townships lying further to the south and west of the main area affected did not show such a marked increase.

Quite clearly then the concentration of population was in the area nearest to Liverpool. In Liverpool itself, growth was proceeding rapidly following upon its development as a port and industrial

In Wallasey, the population grew as show below:-

Year	Wallasey Township	Liscard Township	Poulton-Seacombe Township	Parish of Wallasey	Rate of Increase %
1851	1,195	4,100	3,044	8,339	
1861	1,415	5,625	3,683	10,723	27
1871	1,951	8,070	4,923	14,944	39
1881	1,940	11,612	7,640	21,192	42
1891	2,067	16,323	14,839	33,229	57
1901	4,169	28,661	20,749	53,579	61
1911	9,279	38,659	30,566	78,504	47

From the figures for the Parish, or Borough of Wallasey as it became later, it will be appreciated that between the years 1851 and 1901, the population began to increase rapidly not only absolutely but in the percentage rate of increase. The rate of increase in these five decades was 27%, 39%, 42%, 57% and 61% respectively and few urban areas throughout the country showed higher rates. In the Townships the increase of population naturally was greatest in the two nearest the ferries and Liscard Township, with its two ferries at Egremont and New Brighton and also with a larger area, had a greater population than the Township of Poulton-cum-Seacombe. In Liscard Township moreover the population increased fairly steadily but in Poulton-cum-Seacombe the rate of increase between 1851 and 1881 was so great, possibly owing to the effect on population of the closing down of a number of the industrial works on the margins of Wallasey Pool and the Docks. After this date, however, there was a marked revival of industry involving the establishment of the great flour-milling industry, and the subsequent affect was a great increase in the population of Poulton-cum-Seacombe. In the Township of Wallasey during this period there was a decided lag in growth of population which continued into the early years of the 20th Century. This persisted, owing to the distance from any of the ferries and the inadequate transport facilities until the extension of the Tramway Services to Wallasey Village in 1911.

The Development of Communications

The remarkable growth of population outlined above was in very large measure the result of the provision of increased and better facilities for traveling to and from Liverpool. Outstanding in this respect was the improvement in the ferry services, but, in addition, there were notable development in railway and road transport facilities.

a) **Ferries**

The early growth of the ferries at Seacombe, Egremont and New Brighton has already been traced but in the years 1861-1863 an important change took place in respect of the ownership of the ferries. Prior to this date the three ferries had been run by private enterprise but following upon the Wallasey Improvement Act, the ferries at New Brighton and Egremont were purchased by the Wallasey Local Board from Mr. Edward W. Coulbourn at a cost of £60,000 with an additional £9,000 for boats and stores in 1862. During the following year Seacombe Ferry was bought for £30,000 from the Trustees of Admiral Richard Smith. Henceforward, the three ferries were administered by the local authority. From that time at various intervals, improvements and additions were made to each of the ferries. The fleet of steamers likewise had steadily grown both in regard to the number of boats and in the provision of facilities for carrying a large number of passengers in greater safety and comfort. The chief improvements are indicated under the headings of each ferry.

Seacombe Ferry

Here the first notable improvement was made 1876-1880. In 1876, the old ferry with its "run-out gangway" was closed and for three and half years work proceeded on a complete re-construction of Seacombe Ferry and Approach, on which some £147,000 was spent. This work included the reclamation of land between Seacombe Point and the Old North Reserve Wall (built in connection with the Dock system at an earlier date) on which the now demolished Ferry Hotel and Ferry Approach stand. The re-construction also included the provision of the first floating stage with its gangways and to this was added the hydraulic lift in connection with the luggage-boat service, which remained in use until the floating roadway was opened in 1926. The Clock Tower and associated buildings that remained until re-constructions of 1930-1933 were also built at this time. During this period (1876-1880) a temporary stage was erected against the old North Reserve Wall to function whilst the re-building proceeded. In 1903 and again in 1905 further minor improvements were made at a cost of £11,000 and £5,000 respectively.

Seacombe Ferry, 1880.

Egremont Ferry

At Egremont between the years 1874 and 1876 a new iron pier was built to replace the older wooden structure. This new pier "terminated in a pair of tripods, connected by an arch, which collectively formed a feature familiar on Merseyside for 35 years. On a stone slip. still existing, a run out stage doubled the extensive length of low water landing worked as was the older one, from the whitewashed engine house south of the pay gays, where also was the 'gridiron' on which boats were repaired".

In this condition the ferry remained until 1909 when a sum of £10,000 was spent on the provision of a new floating stage between dolphins which existed until a further reconstruction in 1929-1930.

New Brighton Ferry

At New Brighton, the primitive wooden pier erected by James Atherton remained in use until about 1867 when an iron pier and the first floating stage was constructed. With minor alterations in 1901 at an expense of £3,500, this stage and its bridges functioned until structural replacements were made in 1921 and 1928.

Meanwhile, and supplementary to these great improvements in the ferry stages and piers, a gradual evolution towards the capacious and luxurious ferry-boats was taking place. Reference has already been in an early part to the primitive wooden, single-mast sailing boats that played early in the century. By the year 1856, the fleet consisted of the 'Tiger', 'Elizabeth', 'Wallasey', and the 'Queen of Beauty' all of which were small paddle boats probably ranging up to some 150 tons. The 'Elizabeth' and the 'Wallasey' were constructed of wood and were the last wooden boats to be used on the passenger service. All four had open decks with the main covered accommodation in the form of cabins below the decks. Their engine-power was very limited and breakdowns were all too frequent.

Additional hindrances to the regularly of service were caused through the use of the ferry boats for towing purpose. Even so, conditions were considerably improved on those prevailing during the earlier years of the century. The "Gem" which appeared on the service in 1859-1860 showed but little improvement on the existing boats and is mostly noteworthy in connection with the only disaster of importance into the history of the ferries. This occurred on the morning of 26th November, 1878, when the "Gem" in a dense fog, fouled the sailing "Bowfell" at anchor in mid-river, with the result that the funnel fell among the 250 passengers causing a panic. Many people were pushed overboard and fifteen lives were lost, even though the vessel was not damaged below the water line, and was in no danger of sinking. The beginnings of saloon accommodation were visible in the "Water Lily", 1862; the "Heather Bell" 1865, was the first boat with two funnels and also had a double saloon. In 1884 and 1885 respectively the "Crocus" and the "Snowdrop", the first twin-screw passenger steamers were placed on the service. Each of 300 tons, they had a capacity of 1303 passengers, and in addition to possessing side saloons on deck they had a large smoking cabin below. A few years later, with the arrival of the "Lily" and the "Rose" in 1900, the modern area of screw-built steamers can be said to have been established for, after that date, no more paddle steamers were built.

New Brighton Pier, 1890's

The natural outcome of all these improvements and in particular, the provision of bigger and faster ferry-boats was the speeding-up of the services and a reduction of the fares. Prior to about 1880, the boats ran from Seacombe every quarter-hour until 9pm when a half hour service was carried on until midnight. After that, late travelers had to cross to Birkenhead and from there either had to use a horse-cab or walk. After that year, however, it was decided to institute a 10 minutes service which in many cases meant that the people working in Liverpool could travel back to Wallasey during the lunch-hour.

The combined effect of all these improvements in the ferry services and the resulting development of Wallasey as a "bedroom" of Liverpool and as a sea-side resort, can be judged by the enormous number of passengers carried annually in the early years of the twentieth century. In 1902, the number totalled some 16½ million people end by 1914 this had increased to 24 million. The income derived from the ferry undertakings amounted to £83,400 in 1902 and had risen to £107,700 in 1914. Unfortunately however, in the latter years the increased expenditure on the provision of better facilities together with the increased costs of maintenance resulted in a debit of £4,470 to the Rates of Wallasey.

b). **Wallasey Communication**

The development of land communications and especially of railways in the Wallasey area was very slow. This can be accounted for partly by the natural isolation of Wallasey from the rest of the Wirral Peninsula and partly by the dependence of Wallasey's inhabitants on the ferry services to Liverpool. Between 1840 and 1866 several new lines of railway was constructed on the Wirral. In 1866 the Wirral Railway was built from Birkenhead Docks Station to Hoylake. Wallasey however, was ignored until 1886, when, following upon the opening of the Mersey Tunnel Railway with its attention to Birkenhead Park station, a branch line of the Wirral Railway was constructed to New Brighton via Wallasey Village. Shortly afterwards, an additional branch line was extended to Seacombe Ferry from which station a railway was constructed in the years 1888-1895 running through Bidston, Heswall, and across the centre of the Wirral via Heswall Hills, Neston, Connah's Quay and Shelton to North Wales. The importance of these railways to Wallasey has been limited except in so far as they provided an additional route to Liverpool via the Mersey Railway for the inhabitants of New Brighton and Wallasey Village. In 1903, the Mersey Railway was electrified and this gave some stimulus to the passenger traffic from New Brighton and Wallasey Village but the necessary change at Birkenhead Park from steam to electric trains had militated against the success of this line.

The railway facilities of Wallasey were of very little importance to providing access to other parts of the country outside the Wirral. The services was poor and frequently necessitate changes with considerable delays, accordingly, people travelling to and from Wallasey invariably utilised the main line facilities provided in Liverpool and Birkenhead by the London, Midland and Scottish, and the Great Eastern Railways respectively. There were, of course, exceptions when special day excursion trains were run to Wallasey in the summer season.

c). **Road Transport**

More important in many respects than the provision of railway communications, was the internal development of road transport in Wallasey. The present-day main roads were mostly in existence by the middle of the nineteenth century. Since then, naturally many of them have widened and modernised to meet the requirements of present-day traffic, but the only new main roads of outstanding importance constructed since 1870 were the following:-

Birkenhead Road and Dock Road, which with the Four Bridges and Duke Street Bridge, were constructed in connection with the building of the Wallasey and Birkenhead Docks. These bridges together with Poulton Bridge provided, for the first time, direct land communication to Birkenhead across Wallasey Pool. The value of these bridges, however, was reduced by the frequent delays by the passage of vessels to and from the Docks. Unfortunately the issue is less problematic with the Docks being less used. Poulton Bridge moreover, was a Toll Bridge but had road approaches on either side and consequently was very little used. It was not until the 1930s that the toll was abolished and the road on either side improved.

Seabank Road was extended from Manor Lane across the fields and Magazine Lane to join Rowson Street, thus providing a through route from New Brighton via Egremont to Seacombe Ferry. Prior to this extension about 1860, the chief way from New Brighton to Seacombe was via Rowson Street, Rake Lane, Liscard Road, and Borough Road, an alternative route was from Montpelier Crescent along Mount Road, turning to the right down Mount Pleasant Road and along Seaview Road (then called Marsden's Lane), provided the gates which stood at Hose Side Road end were open, it being a private road.

Belvidere Road, running parallel to, and west of Seaview Road, was constructed partly on an accommodated road leading to Littledale's Model Farm in Mill Lane. From Belvidere Road cross-connections were made with Seaview Road and Claremount Road by Kingsway and Broadway Avenue (formerly Townfield Lane) respectively. These two roads together with Earlston Road provided an east-west route across Wallasey from Rake Lane to Wallasey Village.

A muddy Seaview Road, c1900

Warren Drive, second only in importance to the extension of Seabank Road, was extended in 1880. Until that date, Warren Drive only reached as far as the west end of 'Stonebark' (300 year old house), but then it was extended to meet Grove Road, thus giving New Brighton quicker access to Wallasey Village and the Leasowe Road outlet to Moreton and north Wirral. Originally, it was intended to carry on the road in a direct line to Belvidere Road, which was to be continued across the farm fields to Mill Lane and then along to link up with Gorsey Lane (then also an accommodation road) and so via Duke Street Bridge and road to Charing Cross, Birkenhead. Unfortunately, this scheme for a through route to Birkenhead was prevented firstly by the opposition of a piece of land about Broadway Avenue, and secondly, through the building of houses in Grove Road, facing the present end of Warren Drive. Later, in the 1930's a through route was built on practically the site via Rolleston Drive, Belvidere Road, Torrington Road, Woodstock Road, Oxton Road and Gorsey Lane.

Hose Side Road was made to give access from Grove Road and Warren Drive to the reconstructed Seaview Road.

Harrison Drive opened on 24th June 1901 and provided an extension from the junction of Wallasey Village and Grove Road to the sea-shores.

The net result of these extensions and new road constructions, together with the innumerable small roads built in connection with housing estates, was that the roads and highways under the control of the local authority steadily increased in mileage. This is shown in the following table:-

	Miles	Furlongs
1864	18	6
1670	19	2½
1880	23	4
1890	30	6
1900	36	1
1910	56	1
1914	65	6

Closely related to these improvements and extensions of the roads of Wallasey was the development of the Tramway service. These services became more and more urgent as the need arose to provide transport between the ferries and the increasing and scattered settlements of Wallasey. Although the local authority had obtained power to institute Tramways under the Improvement Act of 1867, nothing apparently was done until 1901. Prior to that date certain services had seen undertaken by private enterprise. The proprietor of Seacombe Ferry Hotel ran semi-public vehicles as far as Leasowe Castle, but they would be intended for the use of visitors rather than residents.

Milnes horse tramway, 1893

Later, in 1879, the Wallasey Tramways and Omnibus Co. laid a single track of approximately two and three-quarter miles running from Seacombe Ferry via Liscard Village to Field Road on the higher ground of New Brighton. This undertaking was purchased in 1901 by the Wallasey Urban District Council for £20,500 including the rolling stock of 7 cars, each capable of seating 34 passengers, seventy-eight horses, stables and tram lines.

Until 17th March, 1902, this horse-car Tramway was successfully operated when it was replaced by the first of the electric Tramways. In later years a number of routes were to the public as follows:-

Rake Lane - March, 1902
Seabank Road - March, 1902
Warren Drive - May, 1902
Falkland Road - July, 1907
Poulton Road - July, 1910
Poulton Road to Wallasey Village - February, 1911

These tramway services effectively linked the various parts of Wallasey with one another and with the ferries; particularly important was the 1911 extension to Wallasey Village which paved the way for the subsequent opening up of that area in the post-war years of the Great War. Their success was assured from the outset and the number of passengers carried annually grew with great rapidity as indicated below:-

Year	Passengers carried in 1000's	Mileage in 1000's	Income £	Credit to Rates
1903	5,685	665	31,470	-
1908	8,331	891	43,820	4,340
1914	13,105	1,291	63,710	7,750

The Four-Fold Character of Wallasey

During the years 1851 to 1914, Wallasey definitely established itself as a town with the four-fold character:-

1. A "bedroom" of Liverpool,
2. A Sea-side Resort,
3. An Industrial and Commercial Centre,
4. A Market-Gardening Region

The importance of each of these roles varies in relation to one another. Undoubtedly, the prize function of Wallasey is as a residential area and the other three functions, although important, are wholly subsidiary and must remain so by virtue Wallasey's position in relation to Liverpool. Moreover, those other functions are very definitely localised in the northern, southern and western margins respectively of the older built-up eastern area. The market-gardening was to disappear with the westward expansion of urbanisation.

1). **Wallasey, a "Bedroom" of Liverpool**

The role of Wallasey as a dormitory of Liverpool had already been indicated in the sections of this part dealing with the growth of population and with the development of communication. Here, it is proposed to indicate briefly the effect of this function on the actual settlement in the area. A valuable indication is provided in the following figures of the growth of rateable value as settlement proceeded:-

Year	Assessable Value £
1845	25,000
1853	35,000
1871	74,000
1881	127,000
1891	161,000
1901	325,000
1911	461,000

Especially noteworthy among those figures is the doubling of the assessable value in the decade 1891-1901, a period that saw a tremendous growth in the building of houses as is seen by comparing the maps showing the built-up areas. The following series of maps indicate generally the built-up areas at the following dates 1841, 1875, 1892, 1902 and 1915. They were constructed by shading in the built-up portions as indicated on old maps of Wallasey and the Ordnance Maps of Wallasey at the respective additions. It is not claimed that these generalised maps are strictly accurate but they are sufficiently correct to illustrate the main trends of building development. The line-shaded areas indicate public open-spaces.

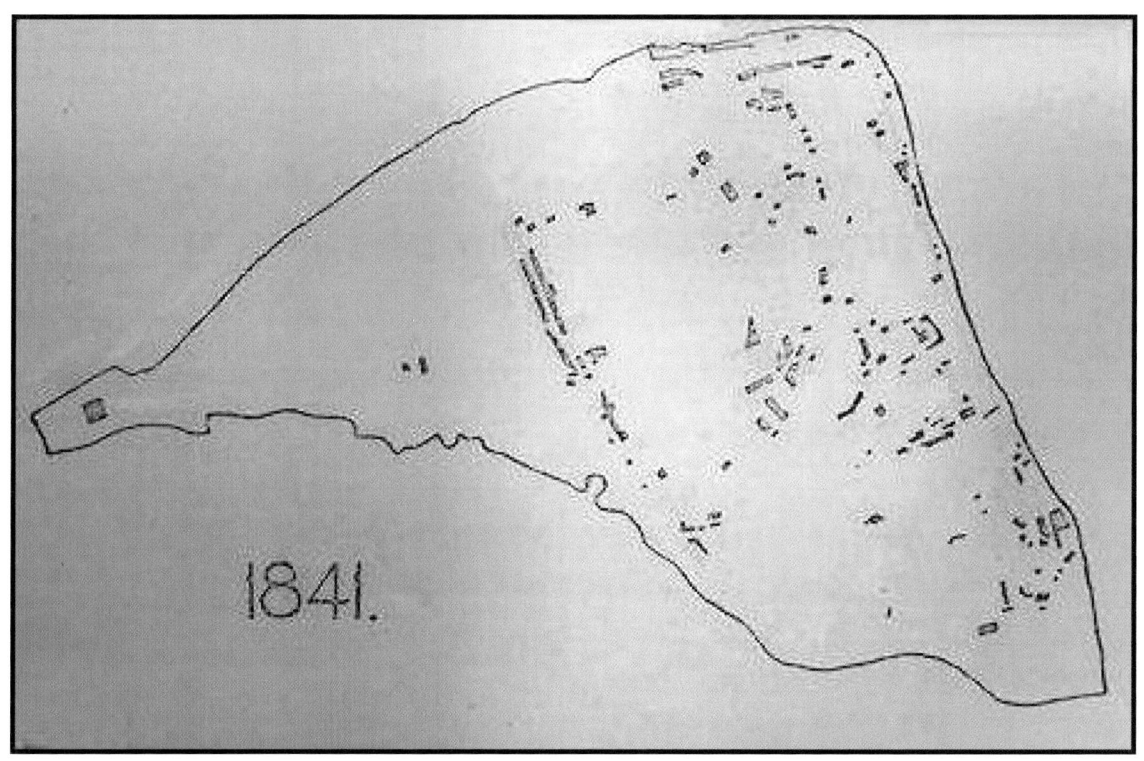

1841.

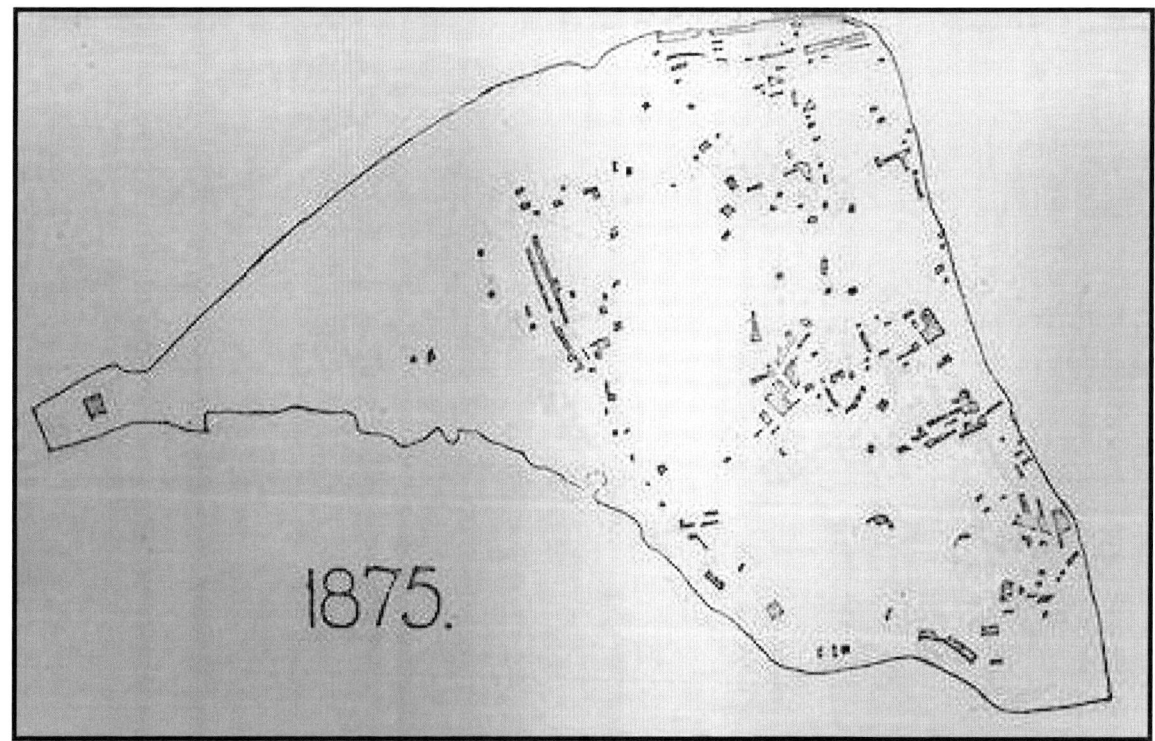

1875.

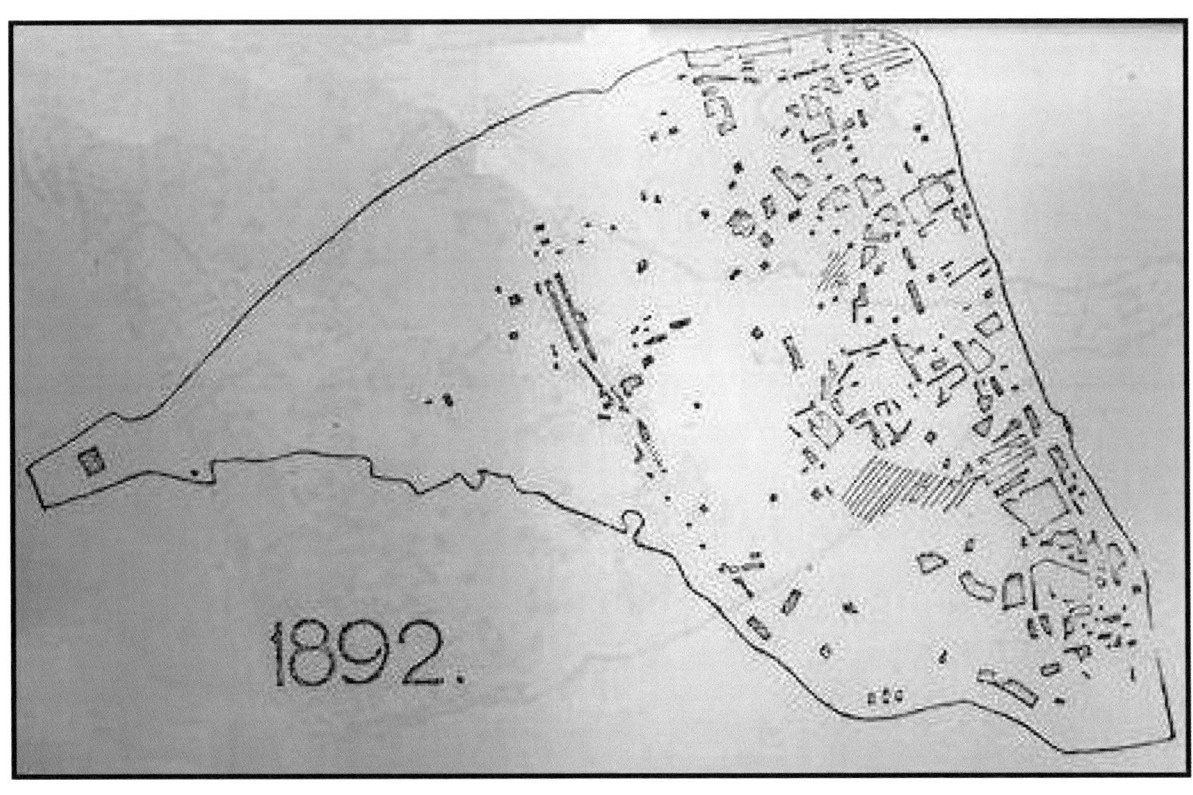

1892.

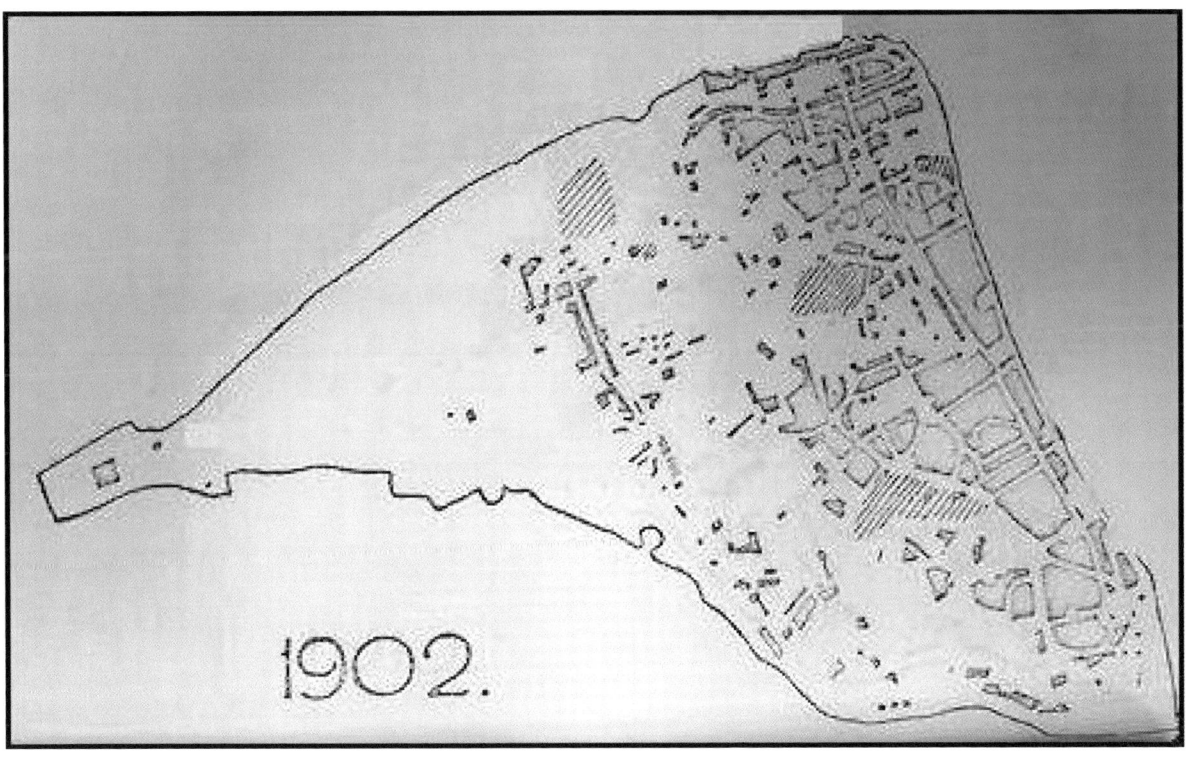

1902.

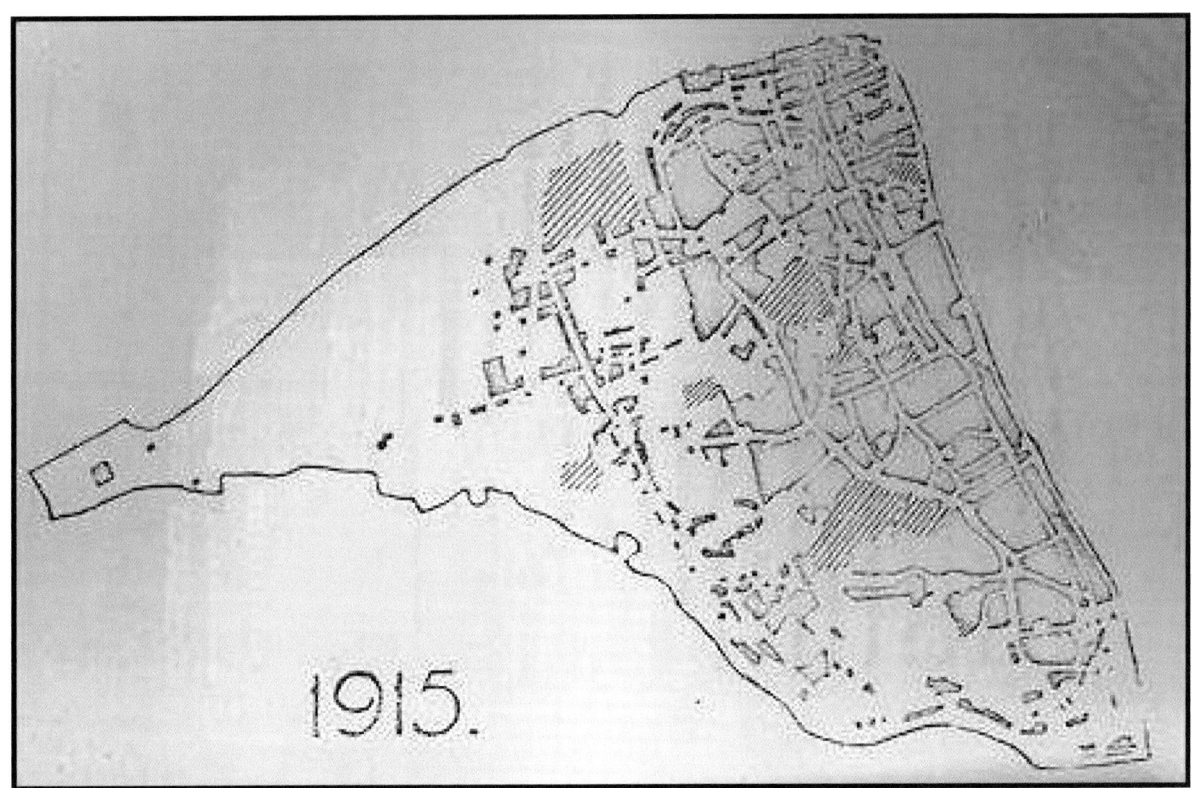

A look at the maps shows quite clearly that the growth of Wallasey has not proceeded from a control nucleus, as had happened in the expansion of so many English towns and Villages. Rather has it been the establishment of a number of scattered settlements separated at first by open century one from another. The hamlets existed by the middle of the 19th Century have been described earlier and consisted of New Brighton, Little Brighton, Magazines, North Egremont, Egremont, Liscard, Seacombe, Somerville, Poulton and Wallasey Village.

Gradually, with certain exceptions, these settlements expanded during the latter part of the nineteenth century, until most of the open country was filled in, and a more compact unit obtained with, however, an almost complete absence of the recognised centre with its administrative offices, business premises and important shops that is so characteristic of most English towns of any size.

Particularly noticeable is the concentration of houses in the eastern part of the Borough, ie. In the districts in relatively close proximity to the river and sea front with their two-fold advantage of proximity to the water-front with the attractions and easy access to the all-important ferries to Liverpool. Even as late as 1915 when the extension of the tramways to Wallasey Village had been accomplished, most of the housing estates lay to the east of a line running along Rolleston Drive, Belvidere Road, Torrington Road, Woodstock Road, Oxton Road, and from the top of Gorsey Lane in a south-easterly direction to the junction of Wheatland Lane and Birkenhead Road.

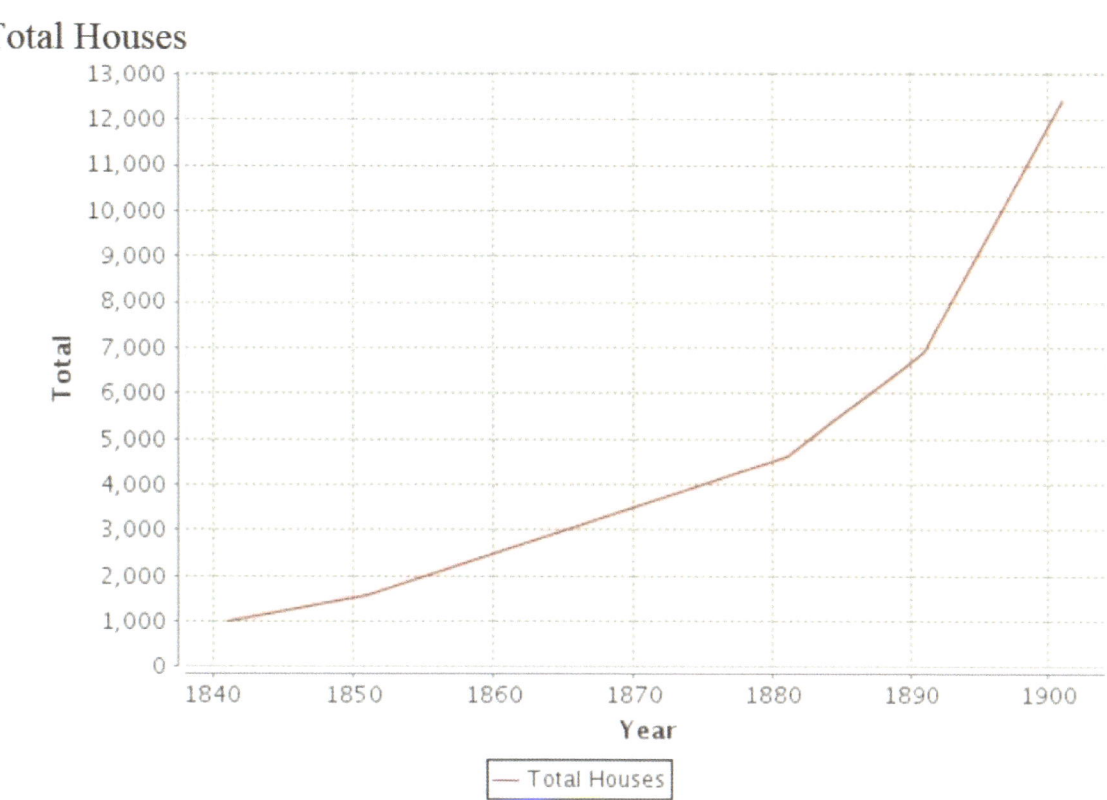

A few instances of the development of housing estates are given in that they are characteristic of the building that was quickly filling up the eastern and elevated portion of Wallasey. In 1870, an open near the old nucleus of Liscard Village, and known as Liscard Park, was purchased and a large number of houses were built together with the laying out of the following roads, Westminster Road, Grosvenor Street, Easton Street, Wilton Street, and Belgrave Street. Then again a few years late, in 1874, following upon a crisis in the Liverpool cotton trade, Mr. Harold Littledale who farmed much of the land in Wallasey, decided to close his Model Farm and sell most of the land.

"It so happened that the Ferry Committee had decided on giving a 10 minutes ferry service to Liverpool from Seacombe in place of the quarter-hourly service. An astute gentleman, Mr. David Benno Rappart, saw the opportunity of providing houses for people occupied in the city, and living in the suburbs of Liverpool who wished to come home for a mid-day meal and get back in the hour allowed. Liverpool was expanding north, east and south, and slow trams prevented this being done. At the same time the Ferries Committee decided to reduce the contract fares to a very cheap level. Mr. Rappart purchased the land between Brougham and Clarendon Road and in a few years the whole of the houses built thereon were let so speedily as they were erected". (Bertram Furniss, 'Memories of Wallasey', Wallasey News, 7th April, 1934)

During the decade 1891-1901, the promenades from Seacombe Ferry to New Brighton were constructed and immediately behind, the open fields were set out with roads and then quickly built up with houses. Here again, the same as Mr. Rappart took a large part in the building developments including property between Holland Road and Manor Road. Meanwhile, considerable land speculation with its subsequent building was going on in the Mainwaring Estate between Liscard Road and Poulton Road. Elsewhere, houses were being built all over the eastern area, at the rate of some six to seven hundred per year. During this increased period of increased housing construction there was a change in the type of brick used. From 1850 until about 1890, plain brick was chiefly used but from then until the First World War it became the general practice to face the houses with that hard-pressed Ruabon brick which presents a good wearing surface but also one that remains harsh and glaring. During the First World War, which practically stopped all building, the cost of Ruabon brick became prohibitive and was no longer used. Another change to be noted in Wallasey during the last century was the almost disappearance terrace-built houses, these being replaced mainly with semi-detached houses.

2). **Wallasey, a Sea-Side Resort**

While the greater part of Wallasey was developing rapidly as a residential area the northern part, fronting Liverpool Bay, was acquiring somewhat doubtful fame as a sea-side resort. The origin of New Brighton and its development were discussed in Chapter 3. Between 1850 and about 1870 New Brighton became more and more popular being regarded as a delightful holiday resort by many of the wealthy people of Lancashire and Cheshire, as Southport, Llandudno and similar sea-side resorts of to-day had not then been developed. It was these gentry who conceived the idea of the promenade-pier and a Manchester syndicate erected it. At first the pier had only one approach by means of a number of steps from the middle of the ferry-pier. When the promenade pier was opened in 1867, it became a great attraction, and in the summer the elite of Liverpool together many of the 'quality' of Wallasey, Birkenhead and the Wirral promenaded every evening thereon. Regattas were held at which some of the finest yachts in the country competed, including many of the competitors at Cowes. Thus for a time, the New Brighton part of Wallasey was a very fashionable sea-side resort, but later in the century it deteriorated to a great degree and became essentially a second-rate resort mainly for 'day-trippers'.

Tea Pot Row, 1869. The row of buildings were demolished by 1871 to make way for the Ham & Egg Parade.

This, perhaps, was more or less inevitable with the growth of Merseyside population and the provision of better and cheaper ferry services, but the change was quickened by the construction of the notorious 'Ham and Eggs Parade' or 'Teapot Row' as it was frequently called. This short parade together with a number of huts to be used as tea shops was constructed just beyond New Brighton Pier, by a Manchester syndicate in 1871. Furthermore, a number of stalls were opened for the sale of fruit, oysters and mussels, ginger-beer, etc, and on the shore horses and donkeys were plyed for hire by people whose swindling propensities frequently led to trouble. On occasion, serious fights resulted as instanced in the following description by Mr. Bertram Furniss :-

> "When the 'Wiganers' came it was certain to end in a free fight; and I have seen 200 or more men lying on the shore and Dr. Bell dealing with them, some insensible, and all bleeding freely from cuts in the head caused by the 'Aunt Sally' sticks which both sides resorted to".

Ham & Egg Parade, c1900

Prize fighting also used to take place on the shore. Generally between one or two of the gypsies and native bruisers. There were also on the shore 'round-abouts', swings and other amusements of the popular type. The 'trippers' spread all over the shore and sand-his and frequently, there was a great deal of drunkenness.

The natural result of all this was that New Brighton acquired a very unenviable reputation and its name spread all over the world carried by the sailors who visited it when their ships docked at Liverpool. Most of the well-to-do, who were the main-stay of the shop keepers during the winter, with their large families and large staffs of male and female servants, generally left the town.

Thus, by the end of the 19th Century, the character of New Brighton had changed completely and for the worse. Further attraction was provided in 1897 by the opening at Whitsundie, of the 'Tower' and 'Tower Grounds'.

Early in the twentieth century, the local authority began to take steps to remove the notorious Ham and Eggs Parade' in order to replace it with a more modern promenade in an endeavour to improve the status of New Brighton both as a sea-side resort and as a residential area. Already, between 1891 and 1901 promenades had been constructed from Seacombe Ferry to New Brighton Ferry. Prior to 1891, the river frontage mainly consisted, in the Seacombe and Egremont sections, of more or less eroded clay cliffs supported by the heavy retaining wall erected some years earlier. This wall terminated about 150 yards from Holland Road and from there to New Brighton the foreshore was contiguous to the boundaries of the various private enclosed properties. Thus, it was impossible to pass from Seacombe Ferry to New Brighton Ferry except via the shore when the tide receded. Consequently, and in view of the building that was quickly filling up the eastern part of Wallasey, the members of the Local Board decided, with commendable foresight, that the river frontage must be made available to the public and visitors, together with as much of the background as possible so as to give an effective setting in the form of plantations, open spaces, and recreation grounds to the proposed promenades. An Improvement Committee was set up and the Promenades were constructed under the Acts of 1896 and 1899. The necessary land and shore properties were obtained after treaty, arbitration and even litigation with the private owners and stage by stage the promenades were extended as follows:

1891 Egremont Ferry to Holland Road;
1897 Holland Road to New Brighton Pier;
1901 Egremont Ferry to Seacombe Ferry;
1906 New Brighton Ferry to Marine Park.

In connection with the last extension, the notorious 'Ham and Eggs Parade' was demolished together with certain property behind and in its place the Victoria Gardens were substituted, these Gardens being formerly opened by Lord Derby in 1913.

The promenades from Seacombe to New Brighton were constructed with a uniform width of 45 feet and were permanently closed to vehicular traffic whereas the section from New Brighton to Marine Park, a minimum width of 90 feet, was an open through fare. A strip of land behind the promenades was acquired in most parts and gradually the following plantations, open spaces, and recreation grounds were set out :-

North Seacombe Recreation Ground, Sandon Gardens, Guinea Gap Baths, Town Hall frontage, plantations north of Egremont Ferry, Mariners' Home Grounds, Vale Park with the adjoining plantations, the Tower Grounds, Victoria Gardens and Marine Park.

3). **An Industrial and Commercial Centre**

Prior to the conversion of Wallasey Pool into the Birkenhead and Wallasey Docks, a number of industries had come into existence in the part of southern Wallasey bordering the pool. These appear to have flourished for a while and then a period of depression followed in the wake of the Dock construction. Thus in the period 1860 - 1890, practically all the industries were closed include the following :-

1860 Sugar Refinery and Smalt Works;
1863 Bibby's Copper Works;
1872 Messrs. Bowdler and Chaffer's Ship Building Yards following
upon a disastrous fire
1873 Seacombe Pottery; about the same time, Seacombe Foundry

and Iron Works, the Cement Works, and the Starch and Vitriol Works, were closed.

The closure of these numerous works would undoubtedly affect the industrial population of south Wallasey but there would be some compensation in the absorption of much of this labour in the Dock constructions and extensions, and in the newly-opened industrial works on the Birkenhead side of the Dock Estate.

The kilns of Seacombe Pottery, 1880's.

In 1857, the Dock Estate had been assigned to the Mersey Dock and Harbour Board and there followed the construction of the Great Float and the Wallasey Low Water Basin, open to the river. During the year 1866, the Alfred Dock was opened and a little later, re-construction converted the Great Float into the East and West Float, separated by Duke Street Bridge. By 1871 there was already a large number of sheds, warehouses and railway sidings in existence mainly on the Birkenhead side and a number of industries were firmly established. The most prominent were the Copper Ore Works, Canada Engine Works, Birkenhead Ore Works, Birkenhead Forge, Wirral Foundry, Britannia Engine Works and the Chain Cable and Anchor Testing Works.

As yet, however, the great flour-milling enterprises that were to play so important a part in the industrial life of modern Wallasey and Birkenhead, were undeveloped although there were grain houses built on the north quay of the East Float. Some years elapsed before the first flour mill, the 'Millennium', was opened by Vernon's in 1899. This inaugurated the Wirral branch of the Merseyside corn-milling industry which had grown steadily ever since with the establishment of more and more mills including Paul Brothers'. 'Home Pride' Mills, Buchanan's 'Silver Queen' Flour Mills, and the 'Wallasey Mills' of Uvecco Cereals.

Further industrial development followed with the opening of the English Process Steel Works about 1905, and the Gandy Belt Works, Wheatland Lane, about 1909. Meanwhile, from 1867 onwards, the local authority had been absorbing more and more labour in the Gas Works, Gorsey Lane, as the output increased in accordance with the demands of the ever expanding population of Wallasey. Thus, in the early years of the last century, a large number of people and more particularly those residing in Seacombe and Poulton, were engaged in the industrial and commercial activities of the Dock Estate and the boarding land. Outside this part of Wallasey, there were no industries of any size or importance with the possible exception of the Wallasey and Moreton Brick Works, in Leasowe Road and Pasture Road respectively.

4). **A Market-Gardening Region**

During the period under review, 1850-1914, part of the low lying land west of Wallasey Village became famous for its market-garden produce. The beginning of this can however, be traced back to the end of the eighteenth century for a certain Thomas Hedge, reporting in 1794 on agriculture in Cheshire refers to the success of market gardens at Wallasey even at that date, saying "the improved method, or what is yet called the secret, of raising early potatoes was first practiced in this country by one Richard Evans, late of Wallasey in Wirral". Later, after describing the method of cultivation, he states "Early potatoes have been as plentiful in Liverpool market for some years past in the middle of May as they used to be in the middle of June".

During the latter part of the nineteenth century, the demands of the increasing population of Merseyside together with the provision of a zone of market-gardening by the pioneering efforts of members of the Deane family and many others. This zone occupied the most fertile area of land in the Borough namely, that part of Wallasey Village between Leasowe Road and Green Lane. Here, the land is low lying and protected from one encroachment of the sea by the sand-hill belt. It slopes very gently towards the Birket or Fender river and has an open, southern aspect. The soil, resulting from the mixture of the blown sand and the alluvial clay, was a light, sandy loam to which has been added repeated application of farmyard or stable manure until now it has the rich dark colour of fertile peat or "moss-land". The presence, in small quantity, of salt in the soil also favours the market-gardening activities.

Climatically, too, the region is favoured. The mild, equable conditions and the relative freedom from frost combine with a fairly even rainfall regime and a slightly salty atmosphere to produce a great variety of vegetables, including early potatoes, asparagus, tomatoes, lettuce etc. Added to these natural advantages of soil and climate, is the protection afforded from the strong sea winds by the thorn or privet hedges that divide the land into small patches. These hedges have been considerably strengthened by the accumulation of hedge clippings and vegetable refuse reinforced where necessary by straw-plaiting to form an almost impenetrable bulwark.

In these market-gardens it was usual to obtain four or five and, on occasion, even six crops per year from the same patch of land. The produce was of high quality and readily finds a market in Liverpool, as it did likewise during the nineteenth century. A valuable market is also provided by the demands of liners and cargo boats sailing from Liverpool. Wallasey tomatoes and, to a lesser extent, potatoes also find numerous purchasers in the London market.

View of the market gardens of Wallasey Village. St. Hilary's Church stands high in the distance.

Chapter 5

Progress In Local Government

The marked growth of population in Wallasey during the nineteenth and early twentieth centuries brought with it a steady growth in the status of the district from the administrative point of view. The salient stages in the evolution of local government towards the constitution of Wallasey as a County Borough can be described briefly as follows:-

1845 Local Commissioners were appointed to undertake the paving, lighting, watching. cleansing, and improvement of the Parish of Wallasey. Population 7,000; Assessable Value, £25,000.

1853 Local Board of Health was created under the Public Health Act of 1848. Population, about 8,700; Assessable Value £35,000. 15 members appointed.

1877 Extension of the jurisdiction of the Local Board for the purpose of the Public Health Act of 1875. Part of the Parish of Wallasey that previously had been included in the rural sanitary district of the Birkenhead Union was transferred to the Local Government district of Wallasey. Population, about 18,500; Assessable Value, £99,885.

1894 Wallasey Urban District Council created under the Local Government Act, 1894. The District was divided into eight Wards, namely New Brighton, Upper Brighton, Liscard, Egremont, North Seacombe, South Seacombe, Poulton and Wallasey. Three representatives were elected from each Ward. Population about 40,000; Assessable Value, £188,550.

1902 Unsuccessful application for Municipal Incorporation.

1910 A Charter of Incorporation was granted by King George V creating Wallasey a Municipal Borough. The Wards were increased to ten and the first Council consisted of 10 alderman, and thirty councillors. Population about 76,000; Assessable Value, £416,515.

1912 Unification, under a Government Order of the Urban Parishes of Townships of Liscard, Poulton-cum-Seacombe, and Wallasey to constitute the Borough of Wallasey.

1913 Wallasey constituted a County Borough as from 1st April 1913. Later in the year, a petition of the Council asking for the grant of Borough Bench was acceded to. Population, about 81,000; Assessable Value, £499, 238.

Following upon the creation of the County Borough of Wallasey, steps were taken to provide a Town Hall and, after the usual battles of sites, the foundation stone was laid by King George V, on 25th March, 1914. Completion was delayed by the First World War and the formal opening only took place on 3rd November, 1920. Faced with Derbyshire stone from the quarries at Darley Dene, it commands a very fine site on the river frontage between Egremont and Seacombe with the main entrance in Brighton Street.

During this period of evolution of Local Government and Administration, much was done towards providing the Public and Private Services and Amenities that are so important in the life of a modern town.

Bidston Foopath, now covered with railway sidings, c1920

Liscard Road junction with Church Street during a carnival, 1920s

Merecroft Avenue, 1927

Poulton Road, with St. Luke's Church just in the distance, 1927

Seabank Road from Lincoln Drive, 1929

Egremont Ferry, viewed from Tobin Street, 1890's

St.George's Park, 1927

New Brighton Pier view towards Fort Perch Rock, 1930

Chapter 6

Wallasey In The Post War Years 1914 - 1939

A Period of Expansion

By the year of 1914, Wallasey had been constituted a County Borough and had established itself primarily as a residential area tributary to Liverpool, with subsidiary, but important, roles as a sea-side resort, an industrial area and a market-gardening region. A period of arrested development followed during the years 1914-1918 when attention was directed to the special problem and activities related to the waging of the greatest and most horrific war the World had ever known. In the succeeding years several pressing problems had to be dealt with and

> "all municipal departments, administrative, financial, educational, trading and non-trading alike had their duties and responsibilities increased either directly by legislation or by sheer force of changed circumstances and demands".

It was a period of reconstruction and of expansion the beginnings of which date from the Local Act of 1920. Even so, a higher administrative status had been acquired in 1918 when the County Borough of Wallasey, previously in the Wirral Parliamentary Division, became a Parliamentary Borough.

The Population of Wallasey

The outstanding problems to be faced were those connected with the remarkable growth of population that has been discussed previously, and, in particular, they included the problem of housing with its related questions of the extension of the Borough boundaries and Town Planning. Before discussing these and other problems connected with the development of New Brighton as an up-to-date sea-side resort and the provision of additional public services and amenities, it is desirable to study the population of the Borough in the post-war years. Especial attention will be paid to the following aspects:-

a). The Growth of Population;

b). The composition of the population;

c). The occupations and movements of the people.

a). **The Growth of Population**

The Census figures of the years 1911, 1921 and 1931 together with the Registrar General's estimated population of 1934, show that a marked change is taking place in regard to the growth of population in Wallasey.

Year	Population	% +/-
1911	78,504	+47
1921	90,809	+16
1931	97,626	+7.7
1934	97,000	-6

It will be remembered that the percentage increases in earlier decades were as follows:-

1871, 39%;

1881, 42%;

1891, 37%;

1901, 61%;

Thus, it appears that from the middle and until the end of last century, the rate of increase was rapidly advancing, but in the early years of the 20th century the rate of increase began to drop considerably, in the census year

1931, the rate of increase was given as 7.7 per cent, but this tends to create a wrong impression in that, during the proceeding decade, the Borough had been extended to include Moreton. In 1926, just prior to the absorption of Moreton, its population was estimated at approximately 9000, a figure that would bring the 1931 population of Wallasey up to 1000,000 when the extension took place. Accordingly it can be assumed that the population of Wallasey (excluding the added area) was already stationary in 1931. Since then, the population had begun to decrease. The decreases is shown as 626 but once again it must be borne in mind that another extension of the Borough boundary had taken place in 1933. By this extension the Saughall Massie area was added with a population of 830, thus bringing the total decrease in population of the 1931 Wallasey up to 1456 or 1.4%. Though the decrease was small it is symbolical of the modern tendency of people to move from the urbanised areas to the bordering rural or semi-urban districts. This tendency is very apparent in the 1926 Density Map of the Wirral Townships which shows clearly the beginnings of the outward expansion of population from the over-crowded north-eastern corner. In general, the areas mainly affected are to be found in North Wirral and in the Dee side districts and more particularly, Hoylake, West Kirby and Heswall. This migration of population from the larger urban areas can be parallel in many parts of the country, as for example, in Lancashire, where most of the large towns, excluding Lancaster and Liverpool show a smaller decline in population during the decade ending in 1931.

In Wallasey, as in Birkenhead, the chief factor accounting for this migration of population, apart from the natural desire of people to live in less congested and more amenable areas, is the provision of better, cheaper and faster means of communication. Improved railway services, the advent of motor buses, private motor cars, and motorcycles make it possible for people to live in the less-populated areas of the Wirral and still be in easy reach of Liverpool where a large proportion have their businesses and occupations. The opening of the new Mersey Tunnel on 18th July, 1934 and the later electrifying of the Wirral Railway lead to a greater migration from Wallasey, Birkenhead and Liverpool.

For over a century, 1830-1939, the growth of Wallasey had been dominated by the provision of better ferry services but now a repetition in modernised form, of what occurred between Liverpool and Wallasey during the nineteenth century, was beginning to take place between Wallasey and the Wirral. Then, over-population and urbanisation together with the development of communications led to large numbers of Liverpool people taking up their residence in Wallasey. These same factors were resulting in the settlement of many Wallasey people in other parts of the Wirral and further afield.

b). **Composition of the Population**

The effect of the marked growth of population during the closing decades can be seen in the census returns of 1911. These returns indicate that of the total population enumerated in Wallasey, only 29.8 per cent had been born within the borough, 26.7 per cent having been born in Liverpool or Bootle. Unfortunately, the returns of the 1921 and 1931 census do not give figures of the birth places and therefore no statistical evidence is available for comparison. However, an attempt was made in about 1934 to confirm the birth-place of some 500 parents of pupils attending the Oldershaw School for Boys, Wallasey. The results then were:-

Birthplace	%
Wallasey	34
Liverpool & Bootle	30
Birkenhead	18
Wirral & North Wales	8
Lancashire & Yorkshire	4
Other places	6

These figures include parents of a number of boys residing in Moreton most of whom were not born in Wallasey or Moreton having come mainly from Liverpool or Birkenhead. Thus, it is possible that the figure of

Wallasey-born adult people will be a little higher than the figure indicated above (34%). When further allowance is made for the number of children born in the Borough and still resident there, the total percentage of people living in the Borough who were born in Wallasey will probably be in the neighbourhood of 35-40%

Movements of Workers and Occupations

An illuminating insight into the fundamental character of Wallasey can be obtained from a study of the Census returns for the years 1921 and 1931. In 1921, the following figures obtained in relation to the movement of workers:-

	Males	Females	Total
Living within the Borough and working outside	13,797	3,942	17,739
Working within the Borough and living outside	1,929	751	2,680
Net daytime decrease in the Borough	11,868	3,191	15,059

From these and other figures, the importance of Wallasey as a residential rather than an industrial area is clearly established. In 1921, no less than 41.1 per cent of the total working population earned their livelihood outside the Borough. (Worth noting the contrast the corresponding figures for the other Merseyside Boroughs which were:- Bootle 35.5%; Birkenhead 27.1%; Liverpool 6.4%). This resulted in a marked decrease in the day-time population, amounting to 16.6 per cent, inasmuch as there was little compensation for the large exodus of workers to be found in the relatively small number of workers coming in from outside.

The areas in which the outgoing workers were occupied together with the origin of the incoming workers are indicated in the diagram:-

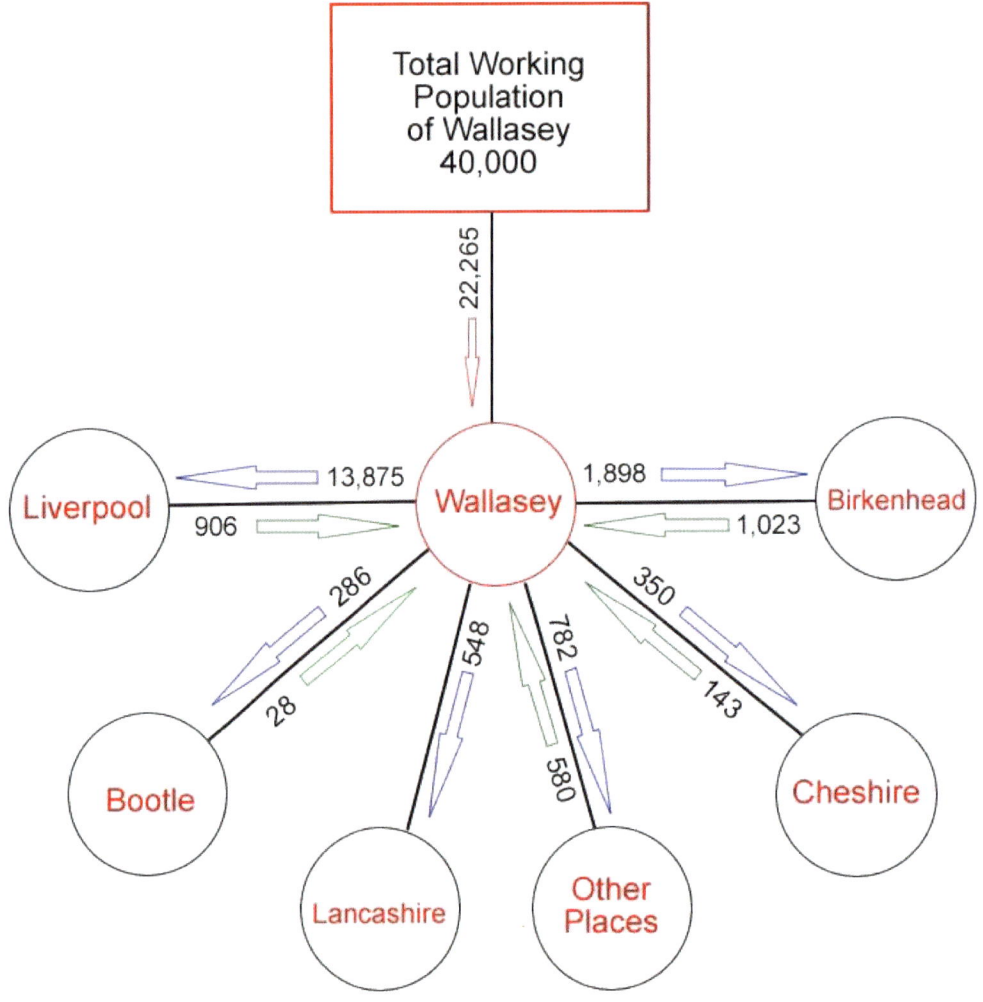

The workers going to Liverpool and Birkenhead were 13,875 and 1,898 respectively and represented 89 per cent of the outgoing population. The movement of people from Liverpool and Birkenhead to Wallasey was 906 and 1,023. Accordingly, in the case of Liverpool the net gain in workers from Wallasey was 12,969 whereas in the case of Birkenhead the net gain was only 875.

The inter-movement of workers between Birkenhead and Wallasey was largely absorbed by the industrial activities on both sides of the Birkenhead and Wallasey Docks, and more especially by the flour billing industry. The more marked outward movement from Wallasey to Liverpool was in 1921, mainly composed of men and women working in the commercial offices and retail shops of Liverpool (as it is today) and provides further proof of the function of Wallasey as a dormitory for Liverpool.

Unfortunately, the 1931 Census Returns do not indicate the movements of workers and comparison, therefore, is not possible. It is very useful, however, to compare and contrast the occupations of the working population of the Merseyside Boroughs in order that the true position of Wallasey in Merseyside can be ascertained.

The varied occupations given in the Census Returns are too numerous for a detailed study to be made here so a classification has been used. This classification divides the occupation into the sex groups given in the following tables:-

Occpation	Year	Wallasey		Birkenhead	
		Male	Female	Male	Female
Group 1. Industrial	1931	31.8	14.3	35.8	20.6
	1921	34.7	11.9	52.9	19.6
Group 2. Transport and Storage	1931	18.3	3.2	24.9	1.9
	1921	22.0	4.0	25.4	8.0
Group 3. Commercial	1931	29.4	28.8	23.1	26.7
	1921	31.5	34.0	14.4	28.4
Group 4. Personal Service	1931	4.8	38.2	4.3	35.9
	1921	2.6	37.6	2.0	34.5
Group 5. Public Service/Admin	1931	11.9	8.2	9.1	8.5
	1921	5.3	2.9	3.0	1.7
Group 6. Professional	1931	3.8	7.3	2.8	6.4
	1921	3.9	9.6	2.2	7.8

Occupation	Year	Liverpool		Bootle	
		Male	Female	Male	Female
Group 1. Industrial	1931	35.5	36.5	33.0	40.1
	1921	43.6	28.7	43.9	32.8
Group 2. Transport and Storage	1931	25.2	1.8	35.9	2.1
	1921	32.7	9.0	37.9	7.0
Group 3. Commercial	1931	23.3	24.5	18.9	21.5
	1921	15.3	24.8	11.6	25.9
Group 4. Personal Service	1931	4.5	24.3	3.7	24.7
	1921	3.1	29.0	2.1	27.0
Group 5. Public Service/Admin	1931	9.0	7.6	6.7	8.6
	1921	3.3	1.5	3.0	1.7
Group 6. Professional	1931	2.5	5.3	1.8	3.0
	1921	2.0	7.0	1.4	5.0

On analysis, the table reveals that in each of the Boroughs the most important group, in so far as males are concerned, is the Industrial Group and that of the 1931 Census, the proportion in each case was approximately one-third of the male working population. This proportion in Wallasey meant that there had been little change since 1921, whereas Birkenhead, to a very marked degree, and Liverpool and Bootle, to a less but still considerable degree, showed a decrease. The post-war depression in Merseyside shipping and industry generally would amount for this decline but in Wallasey the effects of the depression would not be felt to quite the same extent owing to the importance of flour-milling in the industrial life of the Borough, an industry that naturally would suffer less than others in a period of depression. In Birkenhead, on the other hand, the great depression in the ship-building and related industries would account to a large measure for the biggest decrease in any of the Boroughs. In contrast to the regularity of percentage of male workers engaged in industry in the Merseyside Boroughs is the pronounced variation in female labour, ranging from 14.3% in Wallasey to 40.1% in Bootle. In each Borough the number of female industrial workers had increased since

1921. In Wallasey and Birkenhead the increase is very small but it is more clearly seen in Liverpool and Bootle where a number of light industries, such as artificial silk and clothing factories, have been developed during recent years on the outskirts of the urbanised area.

Closely related to the industrial and shipping activities of Merseyside is the group of occupations classed as Transport and Storage and here again a decrease is shown during the decade though it is not quite so marked as in the Industrial group. It is most noticeable in Liverpool and Bootle and applies to both male and female labour. The percentage of females engaged in this group is very low in each Borough and there is a marked similarity between them, much more so then in the 1921 Census. The male labour engaged in this group varies between the 18.3 per cent of Wallasey and 35.9% per cent of Bootle.

Classifying together both the Industrial and the Transport and Storage Groups reveals some interesting contrasts and changes in the four Boroughs during this decade. The figures are given:-

	1921	1931
Wallasey		
Males	56%	50.1%
Females	15.9%	17.5%
Birkenhead		
Males	78.3%	60.7%
Females	27.6%	22.5%
Liverpool		
Males	76.3%	60.7%
Females	27.7%	38.3%
Bootle		
Males	81.8%	68.9%
Females	39.8%	42.2%

In Wallasey, the relatively low percentages of both male and female workers as compared with the other three Boroughs is particularly noticeable. Wallasey also in 1931 shows little variation from 1921. Birkenhead and Liverpool are almost identical. In male workers both the former shows a decrease in female workers while the latter shows a considerable increase. Bootle had a very high percentage of male workers in 1921 and, like Liverpool and Birkenhead, had undergone a decrease. The female labour engaged in these two groups of occupations, already high in comparison with the other areas, had increased still further and is approximately double that of Wallasey and Birkenhead.

The Electricity extension works at Poulton opened in 1926

In Wallasey, by far the greater number of the workers in Transport, Storage and Industry (excluding those few who travel to Liverpool) are engaged in the industrial concerns, with their related transport and storage facilities, to be found in the parts of Wallasey and Birkenhead bordering the Dock Estate.

Some of these industries included United Molaces Co. Ltd, Anglo-American Oil Co., Yelverton Dawburn Co. Timber Works, Uveco Cereals (Spiller's), Vickers-Armstrong Iron Works, Buchanan's Ltd Flour Mills, Gandy Belt Co.

Leather Works, Wallasey Corporation Gas Works, Noris Ltd Oil Refinery, Paul Bros Flour Mills, Currie and Rowland's Manure and Fertilser Works.

Outstanding amongst these industrial concerns were:-

a) The flour and grain mills employed some 1,400 males and 500 females

b) The docks and water transport, employed some 3,000 males - some of these, however, would have had employment on the ships as seamen, pursers, stewards etc.

c) Road and Railway transport workers, almost wholly men, who total approximately 1,400.

d) The Corporation Gas, Water and Electricity Works, employing some 560 men.

The remaining activities in the industrial group were chiefly small in character and a large proportion of their workers was composed of mechanical engineers, motor mechanics, plumbers and electrical engineers.

The group classified as industrial includes several occupations that, in Merseyside as a whole, are of little importance such as Fishing, Agriculture, Mining and Quarrying, and Brick, Pottery and Glass manufacturing. In Wallasey, therefore, it should be noted that the proportion of agricultural workers although small is considerably higher than in any of the other Boroughs.

This is explained by the presence of the market-gardens which provided regular employment for about 250 people with approximately another 250 in seasonal employment, made up largely of women and girls many of whom came from Birkenhead.

Likewise, in regard to Brick-making, Wallasey's percentage is higher than in Liverpool, Birkenhead and Bootle, some 100 people finding employment mainly in the three Brick Works situated in Pasture Road (Moreton), Leasowe Road, and by the Dock Estate in Oakdale Road.

Gandy Belt, 1907

Group 3 consists of people occupied in Commercial, Financial and Insurance activities. Such people as business owners and managers, commercial travellers, shop-keepers, and above all clerks, typists, and shop assistants come under this heading. In general, these people are less restricted in their choice of habitation then the workers in Industry,

Transport and Storage with the result that they tend to spread out to the more favoured localities. The distance from their residence to their place of occupation depending to a considerable degree upon their social and financial status.

In the past, as already stated, large numbers belonging to this group of workers came to live in Wallasey and consequently in 1921, the percentage of the total working population engaged in such activities was considerably higher in Wallasey than in the other Boroughs as regards both males and females.

Most of these people consisted of clerks and typists of both sexes working in the shipping, banking and insurance offices of Liverpool, together with large numbers, more especially in the case of females, employed as assistants and supervisors in the shipping centre of Liverpool.

The growth of 'Football Pools', at this time, such as Littlewood's and Vernon's, also provided seasonal occupation for large numbers of women and girls.

During the period between 1921-1931 the difference in this group became less marked amongst the Boroughs, Wallasey showing a decrease in both males and females (males 31.5% to 27.4%; females 34.0% to 28.8%), whereas Birkenhead, Liverpool and Bootle show marked increases in the male working population and little change in the female.

The slight percentage decline in the male workers of Wallasey engaged in commercial and financial occupations is absorbed in the increased number of people finding employment in Public Services and Administration and in Personal Services. Increased numbers of female workers in Public Services and Administration will likewise account to a considerable degree for the decrease in female workers in commerce and finance. This is further absorbed by the increase in industrial workers.

Group 4, Personal Service, is dominated by female workers, in 1931, only about 4 per cent of the male working population of each Borough finding employment therein. In contrast are the percentage of the females, namely:-

Wallasey 38.2, Birkenhead 35.9, Liverpool 24.3, and Bootle 24.7.

These higher percentages of female workers can readily be appreciated when the types of occupations composing this group are noted. These included the occupations of Domestic Servants and Housekeepers, followed by Restaurant and Cafe Workers, Laundry Workers and Cleaners, Hair-Dressing, Undertaking, and several others.

Obviously, these with a few exceptions are the occupations usually associated with female workers and moreover, they are the types of employment related to residential areas. They can be used as evidence of the residential character or otherwise of the Merseyside Boroughs.

Allowance must be made for the large number of waitresses whose employment in Liverpool is necessitated by the requirements of the daily workers in the business houses, banks and shops. The exclusion of these waitresses will probably reduce the Liverpool percentage of female workers engaged in Personal Service from the 1931 figure of 24.3 to approximately 20.

Comparing the 1931 figures of female employment in this group, it is found that Wallasey takes first place being followed closely by Birkenhead with Bootle and Liverpool well behind.

Accordingly these figures, taken in conjunction with those already given in regard to other branches of employment, indicate the outstanding importance of Wallasey as a residential area. In this connection, Wallasey is a good example of the following observation of E.H Rideout ("The Growth of Wirral"):-

> "It may frequently be observed that in suburban districts occupied by a non-industrial population the possession of a servant is held to be an essential criterion of respectively.

> Hence we find streets occupied by lines of houses quite densely packed together, each with its separate servant, yet whose tenants in similar financial circumstances would, in a manufacturing community, regard such a servant as an unwanted luxury extravagance".

Public Services and Administration (Group 5) and Professional Occupations (Group 6) show little variation between the four Merseyside Boroughs as would be expected seeing that the demand for such is fairly constant in most towns.

Wallasey, however, does show a slightly higher percentage of male and female workers in the professional group. This merely confirms the evidence accumulated to illustrate the residential character of the town.

The demands for professional workers such as doctors, nurses, and teachers being normally greater in residential than industrial towns. Especially noticeable in each of the Boroughs is the marked increase in the percentage of the enumerated working population engaged in Public Services and Administration.

This is not peculiar to Merseyside but applies to all large urban areas throughout the country and results largely from the multiplication of duties undertaken by Local Authorities in the post-war years.

In this group it is noteworthy that Wallasey has a higher percentage than Liverpool, Birkenhead and Bootle, possibly owing to the special problems associated with the rapid growth of the Borough and boundary extensions in recent years that involved the absorption of Moreton.

The relative importance of the different occupational groups in the four Merseyside Boroughs has been discussed and it is now desirable to re-state these, in so far as Wallasey is concerned, in term of actual figures rather than percentages.

Occupations in Wallasey, 1931 Census:-

	Males	Females
Total Population	44,224	53,402
Under 14 years of age	10,176	9,780
14 years of age and over	34,049	43,622
Unoccupied and retired (14 and over)	3,887	29,667
Occupied (14 and over)	30,161	13,955
Out of work	3,898	1,102
Total number in employment	26,263	12,863

	Males	Females
Group 1: Industrial	8,747	1,836
Planning	19	-
Agriculture, mainly Market-Gardening	402	37
Mining, Quarrying etc.	60	8
Bricks, Pottery and Glass	114	3
Manufacture of Chemicals, Dyes, Paint and Oil	655	126
Manufacture of Metals, Machinery & Repairs	1,566	166
Manufacture of Textiles and Textile Goods	92	82
Preparation of Skins and Leather	104	66
Manufacture of Clothing	411	430
Manufacture of Food, Drink and Tobacco	1,642	562
Word Working	351	25
Paper, Stationary, Printing	608	189
Building Trades	1,861	46
Other Manufacturing Industries	297	88
Gas, Water and Electricity	565	8
Group 2: Transport & Storage	4,667	382
Water Transport	1,854	233
Docks	1,146	46
Railways	941	56
Storage	155	14
Group 3: Commercial & Financial	7,545	3,612
Group 4: Personal Services	1,044	4,834
Group 5: Public Services & Administration	2,954	1,044
Group 6: Professional	935	895

These figures, on analysis, show exactly the importance of certain types of employment. Many of the workers are engaged in occupations that are common to all large communities. Enumerated these will include :-

a) considerable numbers of motor-mechanics and engineers, electrical engineers, plumbers, painters and decorators, carpenters, builders and brick-layers. printers, gas and water workers, and others of less importance in the male section of industrial activities; a fair number of the women workers classed as industrial will include dress and blouse makers, milliners, cooks, pastry-makers, and the like;

b) in the transport section there will be road workers such as the drivers of goods and passenger workers such as drivers of goods and passenger vehicles, lorries and vans together with railway workers of all descriptions;

c) in the commercial and financial occupation there will be the usual shop-assistants, clerks and typists, proprietors and managers of businesses, agents, travellers, hawkers and canvassers;

d) the various types of occupations classified as personal services, public services and administration, and professional will likewise, in large measure, be common to all.

Excluding, as far as possible, the above mentioned classes of workers, it will be seen that the chief occupations of the male working population of Wallasey are to be in

1) the industrial and transport activities of the southern part of the Borough bordering the Dock Estate. These provided employment for large numbers in the grain mills, and handling of cargoes in the docks and the movement of cargoes to and from the docks and factories by road, rail and water transport; in addition many were engaged in the ferry services;

2) the commercial, financial and insurance activities of Liverpool.

The female working population, again excluding the larger number finding employment in the local enterprises and domestic services common to most urban areas, is largely engaged in Liverpool. Here, the majority are clerks, short-hand typists, to shop assistants supplemented by those who work in the cafes and restaurants.

In this study of the population of Wallasey from the three-fold view point of its composition, the movements of workers, and the nature of occupations, sufficient evidence has been revealed to prove conclusively the fundamental importance of Wallasey as a residential area (a "bedroom" of Liverpool) with a southern portion devoted to industrial activities and other activities related to a shipping community. Evidence has also been given to show that another district west of Wallasey Village, is occupied by market-gardens which, while covering a fairly large area, do not provide employment for many people.

The remaining function of Wallasey that of the northern part (New Brighton) as a sea-side resort, is difficult to prove statistically. Nearly all this period visitors were accommodated in small boarding houses by the wives of people engaged in Liverpool as clerks, shop assistants and the like. Accordingly, in the Census Returns, these will not appear as Occupied People. Their domestic servants, however, will be classified and these with the waitresses in the cafes and hotels partly will account for the high percentage of Wallasey people engaged in Domestic Service. Furthermore, the amenities at New Brighton such as the Bathing Pools, Tennis Courts, Golf Links, etc, only provide seasonal employment for a relatively small number. (The 1931 Census gave 356 males and 227 females under the heading, 'Entertainment and Sport'. A large proportion of these, however, would have been employed in the local Cinemas). As most of the visitors are day-trippers and come mainly by the ferry services they can be handled by the travel facilities already in existence, in the form of motor-buses and ferry-boats, to provide for the daily movement of Wallasey people to and from Liverpool.

Although the Census Reports are of little value in this connection, there is abundant statistical evidence available in the increased number of passengers carried during the summer season by the ferry-boats and in the number of people using the sea-side amenities especially the New Brighton

Baths and Derby Bathing Pool. The role of New Brighton as a sea-side resort will therefore be discussed in a later section of this part.

Extension of The Borough And The Problems of Housing

The most pressing problem facing the Wallasey Council in the post-war period of World War One was that of housing. The post-war decades had shown a remarkable growth of population that few urban areas in England and Wales could equal. In the decade 1901-1911, only 5 out of the 105 large towns could show a higher percentage rate of increase than the 47% of Wallasey; in the succeeding decade, although the rate fell to 16%, Wallasey was eighth on the list. An inheritance from this period of population growth was the overcrowding in certain parts of the existing built-up area. This can best be shown by an analysis of the density figures:-

Density of people per acre	1921
London (Administrative County)	59.9
Next 12 largest towns	23.0
Liverpool	37.8
Bootle	39.3
Birkenhead	37.2
Wallasey	27.3

These figures indicate that Wallasey, with a much lower density than the Administrative County of London, had a density comparable with the next twelve largest towns. Only 21 of the 79 county boroughs in England had a greater density; large and important industrial towns like Leeds, Birmingham, Sheffield, Cardiff, Nottingham, Leicester and Bolton had a lower density. At the same time, it must be appreciated that Wallasey was the least densely-people of the Merseyside Borough having approximately 10 persons per acre less than each of the others. But these figures with their average for the whole area give no indication of the differential rates of density appertaining to various parts of the Borough. If the Ward densities are substituted, marked contrasts can be seen from one district to another. Even so, the Ward densities are not a completely satisfactory measure of the extent to which people are crowded together or otherwise in that they do not take into account Open Spaces, land used for industrial purposes, shops, special buildings and land not yet developed. By making allowance for such areas and taking only those that are used for residential purposes a much truer statement can be obtained both of the housing density and the number of persons per acre.

The appended table gives both sets of figures:-

Ward	Whole Area		Built0up Area	
	Houses Per Acre	Persons Per Acre	Houses Per Acre	Persons Per Acre
New Brighton	7	36	8	41
Upper Brighton	11	51	13	55
North Liscard	9	37	11	48
South Liscard	16	74	16	74
North Egremont	17	73	17	73
South Egremont	17	73	17	73
North Seacombe	20	104	20	104
South Seacombe	7	39	30	157
Somerville	8	32	25	114
Poulton	5	25	33	136
Marlowe	4	19	22	103
St. Hilary's	7	28	20	68
Warren	3	12	6	21
Wallasey	1	5	21	93

A comparison of the individual ward densities (whole area) with the average (27.3) for the whole of the Borough shows that only 4 of the 14 wards were below the average, the remaining 10 being in most cases well above it. This illustrates clearly the danger of relying on the average figure. In 1921 practically all the western part of the Borough, the low-lying land east of Wallasey Village, was undeveloped consisting largely of open fields, market-gardens and golf links.

The inclusive of this area gave a completely erroneous conception of the built-up area. The ward densities (whole area) indicate that 5 of the Wards had a density of over 50 persons per acre and in the case of North Seacombe Ward the number exceeded 100. High as these densities were, they did not compare with certain wards in Liverpool and Bootle e.g. Netherland Ward (237) and Everton, Low Hill, and St. Domingo each exceeded 150 persons per acre.

A study of the revised figures for the Built-up Area reveals some striking contrasts. In the first five wards, with but limited open spaces and undeveloped land, there is little change in both the number of houses and persons per acre. In South Seacombe, Somerville, Poulton, and Marlowe where large areas were devoted to the Dock Estate and the related industrial works, and densities show a decided increase which was most marked in the case of Somerville and South Seacombe. Somewhat similar increases are indicated for St. Hilary and Wallasey Wards where large areas of land were undeveloped. Warren Ward, although including Harrison Park and the Warren Municipal Golf Links, does not show a very marked increase in the revised figure. This is explained by the character of a large proportion of the houses set in big gardens, the density varying from about 1 to 5 houses per acre.

The over-crowding of people in the houses as well as the over-crowding of houses per acre showed a pressing need in 1921 for steps to be taken to relieve the housing shortage. Here, it must suffice to state that the percentage of population living more than 2 persons per room had almost been doubled in the decade 1911-1921. Comparison with the other Merseyside Borough is given in the following table:-

Year	Liverpool	Bootle	Birkenhead	Wallasey
1911	10.1	9.2	7.6	3.3
1921	12.1	11.6	12.6	5.7

Prices were high and it was well-nigh impossible to obtain a house under any circumstances. Thus, the urgent necessity for attending to the problem of housing in the immediate post-war years was very apparent to all. While some parts of the Wallasey built-up area were quite necessary from the point of view of density others had far too many houses per acre and in certain parts, over-crowding in the houses themselves existed. These unsatisfactory conditions could not be adequately evolved by the enterprise of local builders alone. In common with most local authorities, the Town Council of Wallasey used the facilities afforded them under a succession of Housing Acts and, after 1920, started with the first of several housing schemes.

At first, building operations proceeded slowly owing to the difficulty of obtaining suitable sites at reasonable prices. Further delays were caused by the high building costs of the years following upon the First World War period. Nevertheless, in 1920-1921, the first scheme was completed. This involved the construction of 18 parlour and 15 non-parlour houses in the Alderley Road area. In the next few years further and more ambitious schemes were carried out as follows:-

Under 1919 Act. Mill Lane Estate - 171 houses including 118 of parlour type;

Under 1924 Act. Belvidere Road Estate - 138 houses of a better type and sold to owner occupies. (£750-£760);

Under 1924 Act. Poulton Road - Surrey Street Estate - 56 houses including 26 of parlour type;

Under 1924 Act. Mostyn Street-Norwood Road Estate - 59 houses including 35 of parlour type;

Under 1924 Act. Hillcroft Road-Lyncroft Road-Gorsedale Road Estate - 364 houses including 117 of parlour type.

These Corporation-built houses, supplemented by those built by private enterprises were rapidly filling up the vacant plots of land in the eastern part of the Borough. Even though the number of inhabited houses had increased from 19,503 in 1921 to 21,675 in 1927 the demand was still very great. In that year (1927), although the Corporation list of people requiring houses had been closed for three years, there were still over 2000 people on the waiting list. Most of these required "working-class houses" and the position was very difficult. The newly-developed Corporation Housing Estates had "practically exhausted all the available land in the Borough on which worker's houses could be erected". Hence, it became necessary to acquire authority for an extension of the Borough boundary so as to include the Leasowe and Moreton area.

View of Kirkway from Earlston Road, 1927

Almost of equal importance as the necessity to provide additional building land was the factor of the health of the community. In the Moreton area, lying in the path of the westerly winds that sweep over the elevated eastern part of Wallasey, there had grown up a community of people living in almost unbelievable conditions of sanitation. This 'bungalow' of 'caravan-town' was thus not only a danger in itself but might have become a menace to the built-up area of Wallasey. The origin and growth of this community provides an object lesson of the way in which wholly unsatisfactory conditions of habitation can arise, out of what were originally good intentions, when the development is allowed to proceed with but little control from the Local Authority.

Junction of Limekiln Lane with Poulton Bridge Road, Bird House on the left

Gorsedale Road Council School, 1934

St Hilary Brow, c1905

Wallasey Village junction with Leasowe Road, c1895

Gorsey Lane looking towards Duke Street Bridge, 1925

Gorsey Lane, junction with Poulton Road, looking towards Duke Street Bridge, 1920s

Chapter 7

Wallasey In The Post War Years : 1918 - 1939

The Origin and Development of the Moreton "Caravan-Town"

The following Population Census returns for the Parish of Moreton are very helpful in understanding the origin and growth of the "Caravan-Town".

Year	Population	+ or -
1801	210	
1811	230	20
1821	273	43
1831	247	-26
1841	330	83
1851	350	20
1861	351	1
1871	455	94
1881	424	-31
1891	464	40
1901	597	122
1911	989	392
1921	4,029	3,040
1931	9,082	5,053

From these figures, it will be seen that the population, although doubling itself during the century, remained exceedingly small until the early years of the last century. Clearly then, Moreton remained a quiet, rural, agricultural community outside the sphere of influence of the Merseyside conurbation. At the start of the twentieth century conditions began to change.

In 1900, the Corporation of Birkenhead acquired control of Leasowe Common and in the years following people were permitted to live there in tents during the summer months of the year. These people, coming mainly from the poorer quarters of Birkenhead, naturally derived great benefit from living in the fresh air. Unfortunately the strong winds blowing over the Common caused many people to erect bungalows from 1907 onwards. These bungalows were erected on the understanding that they would be removed when the Wirral Rural District Council so requested.

Under these arrangements the number of bungalows increased until 1913 when complaints began to arise concerning the unsanitary conditions of some of them and the Rural District Council decided to serve notices upon all the bungalow owners requesting that they should be moved. Considerable opposition was raised and in subsequent litigation the bungalow owners won the test case, that of Kerr's Field. This was exceedingly unfortunate for since then the judgement given in that particular "has been looked upon by the bungalow owners as something like a charter of freedom". Further litigation followed and then the war years of 1914-1918 left conditions at a standstill.

In the immediate post-war years, the acute housing scarcity on Merseyside resulted in many people following the example set by the post-war summer bungalow dwellers at Moreton and Leasowe, only in their case, the dwellings were permanent habitants. The influx of people was facilitated by the sale in 1918 of two very large farms in Moreton to land speculators who, in turn, disposed of them in the form of small plots. The consequences were disastrous. They are well described by Sir. Lynden Macassey in his evidence of the 1927 Enquiry before the house of Lords Committee, extracts from which follows:-

> "There became a perfect influx into Moreton of furniture vans, caravans, railway carriages, shacks, and every kind of structure in which a man could live ..... This is what happened, and they exist in hundreds and hundreds. A man would bring a caravan or a furniture van, measuring 6 feet in width and probably 12 feet in length, and in that five and six and seven and up to ten and twelve persons have

been permitted to live ..... One of the worst factors was a complete absence of any sanitary conveniences ..... The denizens of these structures ..... Simply disposal of their slop water by throwing it over the ground around and no attempt was made to dispose of the refused and garbage which accumulated ..... The results is that the sanitary conditions of a great part of Moreton are really indescribable ..... and the result of these sanitary conditions is to produce social conditions of the most regrettable character ..... Many of the roads ..... are nothing more than churned-up earth and it is impossible to walk along many of them without going over the boot deep in the mud, and, what is worst than the mud, the foul water and filth which is allowed to accumulate on these roads as a result of insufficient drainage being provided ..... Actually some of the roads are made up with ashpit refuse, with garbage, so much so that on some of them you can only pick your way as a result of considerate persons who have placed large stones here and there and bits of wood from which you can step in the course of your progress. Until quite recently (1925) no lighting whatever was provided for the whole of this district; there was not even one single public oil-lamp in a district with something like 8,000 persons and an important district, too"

Later, in the evidence submitted to the Committee, extracts were quoted from the 1925 Reports of the Wallasey and Wirral Medical Officers which revealed even more vividly the state of affairs existing in that year. Parts of these extracts are well worth repetition:-

"Moreton demands special treatment in any health report which deals with N.W. Cheshire, not only because it has championed a retrogression to mediaeval conditions, but also because the failure of its experiments must be obvious to all who think" :- **1925 Report of D. Yeoman, Medical Officer of Health for the Wirral**

"If the vital statistics of Moreton are as favourable as reported, Moreton stands as a unique example of the value of light and air in the preservation of health; for if we exclude the influence of light and outside air in my view the worst slum in any large town in all other respects compares very favourably with a large number of the caravans in Moreton; and if there is the urgent necessity to clear away the majority of the caravans":- **1925 Report of Dr. Barlow, Medical Officer of Health for Wallasey.**

Later in his report, the Wallasey Medical Officer of Health goes on to describe the condition of one of the worst fields in the following words:-

"It contained some 150 bungalows in all stages of disrepair, bounded on one side by a foul smelling stench perhaps 2 feet deep, on another by a ditch of about the same depth filled with stagnant water; all absolutely unprotected and crossed by planks in two places. The main places between the bungalows called by courtesy paths were simply churned up and with planks here and there they cross the most perilous parts. Some of the bungalows were actually standing in pools of foul water, while the water had disappeared below others leaving a filthy mud behind. In two spots were placed in the midst of a mass of bungalows the closet accommodation provided for their use. This consisted of whitewashed dilapidated enclosures made of rusty, decayed galvanised iron and wood. In one part of the enclosure, with a concrete floor containing many holes, were placed side by side four pail closets about 2 feet 6 high and therefore, totally unsuitable for children; and immediately behind and within the same curtilage compounds, there were deposited large bumps of petrifying matter of all hints, including human excreta. How such a state of affairs is allowed to exist in the 20th Century is beyond comprehension, and unless one had actually seen, one can hardly believe it possible".

These were the conditions that existed in the period prior to the absorption of the area by Wallasey. The Bill for extension was first proposed and rejected by a poll of the rate-payers in 1925 but on the revival two years later, there was a slight majority in favour of the Bill and, in spite of consideration opposition from the Wirral Rural District Council and others, the Bill became law on 22nd December, 1927. Soon after much was done to improve the conditions.

Kerrs Field, off Pasture Road, in 1925. The dwellers lived in makeshift homes, including bungalows, old railway carriages and old buses. The flooding was frequent and it was said that they went shopping to Moreton in punts!

Roads were constructed, bridges were built over streams, sewers and drainage mains were laid-out and most of all, most of the caravans and bungalows had been removed (2,000 in the first 5-years).

The removal of the caravans and bungalows necessitated the putting into operation of various housing schemes both by Corporation and private enterprise. Accordingly, the Council purchased building sites and erected 200 parlour houses in the Reeds Lane area with a further 322 houses, mostly of non-parlour type, on the Pasture Road site. To these Corporation houses must be added the number of houses of varying sizes built by private enterprises to suit tenants or owners of all classes.

By 1935 these total 487 houses. Many of these houses were built in small scattered groups but three compactly-built areas should be noticed as follows :-

Under 1923 Act	Leasowe Road Estate - an attractive lay-out of 100 houses of 3 or 4 bedroom type, which were sold at the freehold price of £640 and £725 respectively;
Under 1890-1925 Acts	Oakdale Road Estate - 92 houses of non-parlour type and including 24 Cottage Flats. These were built with a view to providing alternative accommodation for the dispossessed tenants of the Mersey Street Unhealthy Area, and Children's Playground was provided in the scheme;
Under 1930 Act	Mersey St. Estate - 72 non-parlour type houses built in 1935 on the site of the demolished Mersey St. Area.

The private building estates vary in size from small ones of 10-50 houses to big ones with 100-250 or more houses. The small areas mainly represent either small vacant patches of land here and there amongst the built-up area or else the sites of large houses which have been demolished.

Examples of the former type are as follows :-

No.	Name and Place	No. of Houses
1	St. George's Park, New Brighton	44
2	Sudworth Estate, Mount Road	49
4	Treforris Road Estate, Gerard Road	14
6	The Willows, Grove Road	36
14	Breck Road – School Lane Estate	16
19	Belgrave St. Estate, Martins Lane	38
31	Bridle Road Estate, Seacombe	20
32	Kent Road Estate, Mill Lane	20
35	Brackenhurst Drive Estate, Holland Road	36
36	Bellefield Crescent Estate, Mount Road	25

Housing Estates of the latter type ie. sites of large houses and their extensive grounds, include the following :-

No.	Name and Place	No. of Houses
9	Clare Lodge Estate, Claremount Road	11
17	Poulton Hall Estate, Mill Lane	26
21	Zig Zag Hall Estate, Seabank Road	33
26	The Laund Estate, Broadway Avenue	22

The remaining estates, chiefly large ones, were built mostly on the open land west of the main built-up area, ie. west of the line running along Rolleston Drive, Belvidere Road, Torrington Road, Woodstock Road, Oxton Road and Gorsey Lane. The following are the larger estates :-

No.	Name and Place	No. of Houses
3	Oarside Estate, Mount Pleasant Road	114
5	Green Lane Estate	112
7	St. George's Road- Claremount Road Estate	266
8	Rolleston Drive – Claremount Road Estate	250
20	Ripon Road – Sandy Lane Estate	151
30	Breck Hey Estate, Wallasey Road	219
33	Palmerston Road – Marlowe Road Estate	503
39	Mosslands Drive Estate, off Leasowe Road	156
41	Gorsey Lane Estate	132

The majority of these houses were built 12 to the acre, the outstanding exception being the Gorsey Lane Estate. This Estate, situated in the southern part of Wallasey near the industrial zone, consisted of working-class houses with a density of 18 per acre.

Over the next few years further estates were built in Green Lane, Leasowe Road and Reeds Lane, as well as over a great part of Moreton. Accordingly, the control vested in the Local Authority by the recent Town Planning Acts became important in the preservation of amenities and the provisions of roads, open-spaces and the like.

Bellefield Estate, 1927

St. George's Park, 1927

The Willows, 1927

Lymington Road, 1927

The Post-War Development of New Brighton

The Wallasey Corporation Bill of 1927 not only included the extension of the Borough boundaries, it gave the Local Authority power to proceed with the construction of promenades and the related Baths and Boating Lake that made a marked difference in the importance of New Brighton as a seaside resort. These changes inaugurated a new era in the life of the northern part of the Borough.

The decline of New Brighton as a notable resort towards the end of the 19th Century has been covered in a previous chapter together with the attempts of the Corporation to rehabilitate it by the substitution of a new promenade and the Victoria Gardens and Marine Park in place of the notorious 'Ham and Eggs Parade'. Beneficial as these improvements were they did little or nothing to change the fundamental role of New Brighton as a "day-tripper" resort. Proximity to the big towns and industrial centres of Liverpool and Birkenhead with the consequent cheapness and rapidity in reaching New Brighton have made it a day-time resort for the peoples of these towns and more particularly the working-class people and their children. On reasonably fine days in summer, large numbers of these came by ferry, or by bus in the case of Birkenhead, and on Bank Holidays there was a tremendous influx of such visitors. The following statistical averages concerning passengers carried on the three ferry services in the mid 1930's are very illuminating in this respect:-

Summer and Winter Daily and Monthly Variations		
Month	Turnstile Daily	Passenger Monthly
July	39,193	1,608,739
December	20,296	618,427
Increase: Summer over Winter	18,897	996,312

Average Number of Passengers at the Bank Holiday Period		
Easter	Whitsuntide	August
354,000	266,000	346,000

The general statistics show that for the five seasonal months of the year, May to September, the average number of ferry passengers is 750,000 per month means that approximately 275,000 enter the district as "trippers", the regular daily passengers as contract holders being in addition to these numbers. To these of course, must be added the large numbers brought by bus from Birkenhead and by charabanc and train on day-trips from further afield.

While realising the importance of this function as a play-ground and resort for the working class people of the immediate neighbourhood, the Merseyside conurbation, the Corporation of Wallasey, stimulated no doubt by the desires of the Boarding-House and Shop Keepers of New Brighton, spent over £1,000,000 on facilities for recreation and amusement that attracted many period-visitors to the district and placed New Brighton among the foremost sea-side resorts of Northern England.

In the 1930's various schemes were accomplished including :-

1. The extension of the Promenade from Marine Park to Harrison Drive which included the Marine Lake.

2. Marine Lake of 10 acres utilised for rowing-boats, motor-boats, and miniature motor-boats for children. Already, from the two summers following its opening in 1934, over 1,000,000 people had used it.

3. New Brighton Bathing Pool, the World's largest open-air bathing pool with accommodation for 2,000 bathers and 10,000 spectators. Opened on the 15th June 1934, it was used during the remainder of that summer by approximately a quarter of a million bathers and these combined with spectators to bring the total number of visitors to only a few hundreds short of a million.

4. A capacious car park, in the immediate vicinity of the Bathing Pool and Boating Lake.

5. Sunken Gardens with Tennis Courts, Bowling Greens, Putting Greens, etc.

In addition, the New Brighton Pier was purchased from a private company in 1928 and after a complete reconstruction was opened with an attractive promenade and cafe, lounge, band-stand and Yacht Club premises. At the Harrison Drive part of the sea-front, the Derby Bathing Pool was opened in 1932 and provision was made for residents and visitors alike in the construction of Beach Chalets. Shelters, Cafes and other similar amenities.

The effects of these additions to the existing sea-side amenities of the northern part of the Borough had been considerable. The old appeal that New Brighton had for "day-trippers" had been enhanced. In this connection, the other factors must be borne in mind, namely :-

1. The remarkable development of motor charabanc day-trips in the post-war years of the Great War. Since the opening of the New Brighton Baths charabanc parties had come from most parts of Lancashire, Cheshire, the Potteries and the Midland;

2. The opening of the Birkenhead Mersey Tunnel. This in itself had greatly facilitated communications by road from Lancashire and the North and was greatly used by motorists, cyclists, and charabancs in reaching New Brighton.

Although the influx of day visitors had been more marked than ever, there has also been some improvement in the number of period-visitors.

The Provision of Public and Private Service and Amenities

During the post-war period considerable changes and improvement had been made in regard to the provision of the public services and amenities that were necessary in any urban community. A detailed analysis of these developments is not essential here, that is rather the province of a social survey of the Borough, but certain of the main features can be indicated under their respective readings.

I. **Transport Services**. In this connection, the chief facts to be considered are concerned with the provision of better means of internal communication within the Borough, and especially from various in the ferry services themselves.

a). The Ferry Services have been greatly improved by the provision of additional and more powerful ferry-steamers including the following:-

Year	Names	Capacity
1927	"Wallasey" and "Marlowe"	2,225
1932	"Royal Iris II"	2,000
1934	"Royal Daffodil II"	2,000

Meanwhile, improvements were being carried out at each of the three landing stages and approaches. At Seacombe in 1926, a new landing stage and a three track Floating Roadway were installed at a cost of £204,000 to overcome the difficulties or transporting vehicular traffic. Later, between the years 1930-1933, work on a new Terminus was completed at Seacombe which resulted in the doubling of the dimensions of the Main Booking Hall and of the large Gangway bridges. The new buildings also provided the necessary offices, an extensive covered park for motor cars, and covered approaches to the bus loading stations. The new terminus was officially opened on 19th April 1933. At Egremont Ferry, certain reconstructions that had been carried out in 1929 were rendered useless for a period through a large steamer, 'British Commander', collided with and destroyed the pier in 1932. Since then, however, a new structure had been placed in position which included a new bridge of 160 feet length. Egremont pier reopened on 1st August 1933. Somewhat similar improvements were carried out at New Brighton Ferry in 1934 when a large new passenger bridge was installed.

Thus, in every possible way, the Local Authority had strived to keep pace with the demands of modern Wallasey in regard to the provision of water-transport services to and from Liverpool both as regards passenger and vehicular traffic and in the interest of residents and visitors alike.

b). Road Transport, in similar fashion, had kept pace with modern requirements for speed, comfort and safety in so far as Public Services were concerned. The Tramway Services, the origin and development of which were outlined in Chapter 4 were gradually replaced by motor-buses running along the same and other additional routes. In particular, the new routes, besides facilitating movement in the existing built-up-area, provided services to link up with the newly added of Leasowe and Moreton with the eastern area and the ferries. Through inter-communication with Birkenhead was provided by the joint services instituted between Seacombe Ferry and Charing Cross and between Liscard Village and Charing Cross. These services, began in 1921, were added to in 1929 by an additional joint-service between New Brighton and New Ferry.

In 1935, the route mileage operated amounted to some 31 miles and the fleet of buses consisted of 11 single deck and 83 double-deck covered vehicles. All parts of the Borough were now served by some fifteen routes. Most of these routes were connected with the three ferries and more particularly with Seacombe Ferry where in rush hours, with all vehicles available, the frequency of the bus services varied from two to ten minutes.

II. **Water, Gas and Electricity Services.**

Following upon the rapid expansion of population in Wallasey during the nineteenth and early twentieth centuries the demands for such services as the supplying of water, gas, and electricity steadily increased.

a). The Water Supply was first commenced in 1858 when the Wallasey Commissioners obtained powers to construct water works at Poulton where the first well was sunk and pumping engines installed in 1859, at which date the Water Tower in Mill Lane was commenced. Prior to this date, the inhabitants of Wallasey had upon various streams and private wells at different spots in the district. The water obtained from this first public-supply well was very unsatisfactory owing to the high sand content. A fresh well was sunk adjoining the first and later, in 1872, an additional well was bored at Poulton. Until 1894, these two wells constituted the whole supply of the district but in that year Liscard Pumping Station was opened on a site near Seaview Road (where ASDA stands today).

As time passed and the demands of the populace increased negotiations with Liverpool Corporation and later with Birkenhead Corporation resulted in the provision of further water supplies from the reservoirs of these two authorities at Lake Vyrnwy and Lake Alwen respectively. By these negotiations large supplies of pure and soft water were obtained and mixed with the hard, pumped water from the local New Red Sandstone. The supply from Liverpool was to extend over a period of 30 years terminating

1935. Accordingly, from August 1935, the supply was stopped and the deficiency was met by obtaining additional supplies both of soft water from the Birkenhead source and hard water from the local wells. This latter supply has necessitated the construction of a Water Softening Chemical Process Plant.

b). Gas and Electricity Supply. The provision of a public gas supply dates back to 1860 and since that date at varying intervals improvements and additions were made which included the Gas Works in Gorsey Lane. The public supply of electricity naturally is of later origin and may be said to have begun in January 1897, when current was supplied for lighting from a single-phase generating station at Seaview Road. The demands for additional power in connection with the development of electric Tramways and industrial concerns resulted in the building of a new Generating Station in Dock Road, Poulton, the plant of which started up in August 1915. By 1934 the operation came under the control of the Central Electricity Board under the National Grid Scheme.

c). Schools and Libraries

These essential social services were provided by the Local Authority in accordance with the requirements of a residential area such as Wallasey.

Coronation Avenue, 1945

By 1861, there were five National Schools, each attached to a Church of England. Other Church Schools at that date included St. Alban's Catholic School, the Seacombe Wesleyan School and the one founded by the Calvinistic Methodist.

Further developments took place during the century, especially after the 1876 Elementary Education Act, but the most important construction of Schools followed upon the creation of the Local Education Authority for Elementary Education, under the 1902 Education Act. Since that date the following new Council Schools or extensions to existing schools have been built and opened :-

Manor Road	1905
St. George's Road	1907
Poulton	1908
Vaughan Road	1908
Higher Elementary	1908
Extension to Somerville	1912
Church Street	1916
Egerton Grove	1928
Barnston Lane, Moreton	1930
Extensions to Upton Road	1931
Alterations to Manor Road	1932
Gorsedale Road	1934
Alterations to Somerville	1934
Catholic School, Moreton	1935
Coronation Avenue	1938

Considerable attention had also been given to Secondary Education in the Borough. The Grammar School moved to the Withen's Lane site in 1911 and was enlarged over time. The High School For Girls acquired the Mount Pleasant Road premises and opened in 1909.

In 1919 the Borough decided to take responsibility for the disabled children of the parish by taking over a special school in Lucerne Road, which had been run by the Children's Aid Association.

Initially the plan was to move the school to a new one in Walkers Croft, off St. Georges Road, but the plan was dropped and in 1928 the school was transferred to the large mansion Ellery Park.

In 1920 the old Town Hall in Church Street, Egremont, which had been built in 1873 and later to be heavily damaged during a German air-raid in World War II, became a centre for the evening classes transferred from Wallasey Grammar School.

In the same year saw the delayed opening of the Oldershaw School for Boys and Girls in premises that originally were intended for Council Schools. There was also a Secondary Girls School in Rowson Street, the Maris Stella Convent School which was organised by the Catholic body of that name.

Other important educational activities included the School of Art in Central Park, aswell as a comprehensive system of evening classes.

The Hadow Report in 1926 advocated new organisaton of separate schools for all children over the age of eleven. In consequence of this new policy Gorsedale Senior School was built in 1934; and in the same year Church Street Elementary School, which had been built in 1916, became a Juniors Boys, Junior Girls' and Infants School.

One of the earliest Board Schools, Riverside, which had been 'all-standard', was also reorganised as two Junior Schools and an Infants' School. The last school to open during this period was Eastway Council School (Eastway Primary School today) which opened in 1939.

Libraries

Wallasey in the 1930's had a number of libraries:-

1. a large Central Library in Earlston Road, containing Lending and Reference Libraries and the usual facilities for quiet reading, for lectures and the like;

2. the South Branch Library, in Borough Road, Seacombe.

3. a small branch in Wallasey Village; and

4. another small branch in Moreton.

d). Open Spaces and Recreational Facilities

During the closing years of the nineteenth century the local authority took steps to acquire certain patches of land for the purpose of Open Spaces and to provide recreational facilities for the growing population. By the 1930's there were 32 public parks, commons and other open spaces of a total of 313 acres. The existing areas varied in size from about ½ acre in the small recreation grounds to the 56 acres of Leasowe Common.

In these parks and other open spaces there is the following provision for playing organised games:-

Football	22 pitches in 6 parks
Cricket	4 pitches in 2 parks
Hockey	4 pitches in 2 parks
Tennis (hard court)	19 courts in 3 parks
Tennis (grass court)	4 courts in 3 parks
Bowling	20 greens in 6 parks
Putting	2 greens in 1 park
Children's Playgrounds	9 grounds in 8 parks

Apart from these public facilities there was also the Warren Municipal Golf Course and innumerable private tennis courts, the Wallasey and Leasowe Golf Links and nearby, the West Cheshire and Bidston Golf Links.

e). Shopping Areas.

In regard to the number of shops Wallasey was more than abundantly provided for. The district had many small groups of shops or single shops scattered about. Many of these shops were converted houses which grew as the residential areas grew. However, there was a ratio of 1 shop per 10 persons which was far too high in the interests of both shop-keepers and local populace. This resulted in shops changing hands many times or standing empty for long periods.

A factor of marked importance in the understanding of the problems related to shopping areas in Wallasey is that of the competition affected by the close proximity of the Liverpool shopping district (as again seen today with Liverpool One). The effect of this can readily be appreciated when it is pointed out there was only one shop (Liscard branch of the Birkenhead and District Co-operative Stores) of any size or magnitude in the whole of the Borough with a population of nearly 100,000 people. Most towns of similar size elsewhere have a regional function to perform in respect to trade as also in respect to other aspects of their economic and cultural life. Consequently, they usually have large shops that are a magnet to the house-wives for miles around.

Wallasey had no function of this character, other than as a playground or sea-side resort for the Merseyside conurbation; it was overshadowed by Liverpool. Thus apart from the ordinary everyday requirements provided by the dairies, butchers, grocery stores and many others, the Wallasey people relied to a great extent upon the large trading houses and shops such as Lewis's, Blackler's, Owen Owen's, the Bon Marche and Cooper's. These concerns with their large turn-over can offer goods for sale frequently at lower prices than the small Wallasey shops. An added attraction, of course, was the greater quality of goods they can display.

Furthermore, associated with shopping was the feeling of having a "day's outing' (as is today with a visit to Cheshire Oaks) which provided a break in the house-wife's usual routine of domestic activity. Many utilise the opportunity to visit a Liverpool Cinema or Theatre either at a matinee performance or, after meeting their husbands who were usually working in Liverpool, at an evening performance.

In the 1930s better transportation between the Wirral and Liverpool, the Mersey Tunnel being the most important of these changes, meant most of the big shops could offer daily or weekly deliveries with Wallasey.

A view of Wallasey Road in 1936 with St. Alban's Road to the right. Central Market is on the left and the old Wellington Pub is in the distance

Liscard went through a major regeneration in the 1930s. One of the main new features was the building of Coronation Buildings in Wallasey Road which opened in 1938. Previously the site was private dwellings and Central Market. The Market was built in the 1920s and had many stalls which sold meat, fruit, vegetables, fancy goods and secondhand books.

Other books by the author

- The Story of Old Seacombe
- Wallasey Old Adverts
- A View From The Tower : Stories of Old Wallasey
- The 1938 Wallasey Trade Directory

Printed in Great Britain
by Amazon